29

INTRODUCING
ISSUES WITH
OPPOSING
VIEWPOINTS®

Religion in Schools

Other books in the Introducing Issues
with Opposing Viewpoints series:

AIDS
Civil Liberties
Cloning
The Death Penalty
Gangs
Gay Marriage
Genetic Engineering
Smoking
Terrorism

INTRODUCING
ISSUES WITH
OPPOSING
VIEWPOINTS®

Religion in Schools

Noël Merino, *Book Editor*

Christine Nasso, *Publisher*
Elizabeth Des Chenes, *Managing Editor*

GREENHAVEN PRESS
An imprint of Thomson Gale, a part of The Thomson Corporation

THOMSON
━━━━✦━━━━ ™
GALE

Detroit • New York • San Francisco • New Haven, Conn. • Waterville, Maine • London

THOMSON
GALE

379.28 RELIGIO 2008

Religion in schools

LIBRARY OF CONGRESS CATALOGING-IN-PUBLICATION DATA

Religion in schools / Noël Merino, book editor.
   p. cm.—(Introducing issues with opposing viewpoints)
   Includes bibliographical references and index.
   ISBN-13: 978-0-7377-3850-6 (hardcover)
   1. Religion in the public schools—United States.   I. Merino, Noël.
   LC111.R47 2007
   379.2'8—dc22

                                                              2007036334

ISBN-10: 0-7377-3850-2 (hardcover)

Contents

Chapter 3: Should Public Schools Allow School Prayer?

Foreword

Indulging in a wide spectrum of ideas, beliefs, and perspectives is a critical cornerstone of democracy. After all, it is often debates over differences of opinion, such as whether to legalize abortion, how to treat prisoners, or when to enact the death penalty that shape our society and drive it forward. Such diversity of thought is frequently regarded as the hallmark of a healthy and civilized culture. As the Reverend Clifford Schutjer of the First Congregational Church in Mansfield, Ohio, declared in a 2001 sermon, "Surrounding oneself with only like-minded people, restricting what we listen to or read only to what we find agreeable is irresponsible. Refusing to entertain doubts once we make up our minds is a subtle but deadly form of arrogance." With this advice in mind, Introducing Issues with Opposing Viewpoints books aim to open readers' minds to the critically divergent views that comprise our world's most important debates.

Introducing Issues with Opposing Viewpoints simplifies for students the enormous and often overwhelming mass of material now available via print and electronic media. Collected in every volume is an array of opinions that capture the essence of a particular controversy or topic. Introducing Issues with Opposing Viewpoints books embody the spirit of nineteenth-century journalist Charles A. Dana's axiom: "Fight for your opinions, but do not believe that they contain the whole truth, or the only truth." Absorbing such contrasting opinions teaches students to analyze the strength of an argument and compare it to its opposition. From this process readers can inform and strengthen their own opinions, or be exposed to new information that will change their minds. Introducing Issues with Opposing Viewpoints is a mosaic of different voices. The authors are statesmen, pundits, academics, journalists, corporations, and ordinary people who have felt compelled to share their experiences and ideas in a public forum. Their words have been collected from newspapers, journals, books, speeches, interviews, and the Internet, the fastest growing body of opinionated material in the world.

Introducing Issues with Opposing Viewpoints shares many of the well-known features of its critically acclaimed parent series, Opposing Viewpoints. The articles are presented in a pro/con format, allowing readers to absorb divergent perspectives side by side. Active reading questions preface each viewpoint, requiring the student to approach the material thoughtfully and carefully. Useful charts, graphs, and cartoons supplement each article. A thorough introduction provides readers with crucial background on an issue. An annotated bibliography points the reader toward articles, books, and Web sites that contain additional information on the topic. An appendix of organizations to contact contains a wide variety of charities, nonprofit organizations, political groups, and private enterprises that each hold a position on the issue at hand. Finally, a comprehensive index allows readers to locate content quickly and efficiently.

Introducing Issues with Opposing Viewpoints is also significantly different from Opposing Viewpoints. As the series title implies, its presentation will help introduce students to the concept of opposing viewpoints, and learn to use this material to aid in critical writing and debate. The series' four-color, accessible format makes the books attractive and inviting to readers of all levels. In addition, each viewpoint has been carefully edited to maximize a reader's understanding of the content. Short but thorough viewpoints capture the essence of an argument. A substantial, thought-provoking essay question placed at the end of each viewpoint asks the student to further investigate the issues raised in the viewpoint, compare and contrast two authors' arguments, or consider how one might go about forming an opinion on the topic at hand. Each viewpoint contains sidebars that include at-a-glance information and handy statistics. A Facts About section located in the back of the book further supplies students with relevant facts and figures.

Following in the tradition of the Opposing Viewpoints series, Greenhaven Press continues to provide readers with invaluable exposure to the controversial issues that shape our world. As John Stuart Mill once wrote: "The only way in which a human being can make some approach to knowing the whole of a subject is by hearing what can be said about it by persons of every variety of opinion and studying all modes in which it can be looked at by every character of mind. No wise man ever acquired his wisdom in any mode but this." It is to this principle that Introducing Issues with Opposing Viewpoints books are dedicated.

Introduction

"The Constitution guarantees freedom of religion, not freedom from religion."

—Elizabeth Dole

The subject of religion in public schools has always been a contentious issue in the United States. While many people agree with the general principle that people ought to be free to practice their religion, exactly what this actually means is hotly debated. In the quote above, from a speech given at the Republican National Convention in 2004, Elizabeth Dole emphasizes the value of allowing people the freedom to exercise whatever religion they choose, but undermines the value of being free from religion. The freedom to practice one's religion, after all, rests on both the freedom to engage in one's own religious practices as well as the ability to have freedom from the imposed religious practices of others. Where to draw the line on certain policies that affect freedom of religion, such as the policies that public schools adopt, is an issue of dispute.

One example of this tension between the two values can be seen in the issue of Bible classes in public schools. Currently, many public schools have a course that uses the Bible in some manner. Is there a way to use the Bible in a public school course that does not establish religion nor inhibit religion? Depending on one's point of view, one may find different answers to this question.

In 2007 in Odessa, Texas, some residents, aided by the American Civil Liberties Union and the People for the American Way Foundation, filed a federal lawsuit claiming that the elective Bible course offered by the Texas public schools violated individual religious liberties. The course, created by the private organization National Council on Bible Curriculum in Public Schools (NCBCPS) is called The Bible in History and Literature and was first taught in two high schools in Odessa, Texas, during the 2006–2007 school year. Among the charges in the lawsuit are that this particular course "impermissibly conveys a message of endorsement of religion generally and a particular interpretation of one form of Protestant Christianity specifically" and "advocates particular religious viewpoints to guide the lives of students."

Some people, like Bart Ehrman, University of North Carolina professor and biblical scholar, believe studying the Bible is an important part of education for everyone. "I think for any educated person, it's absolutely essential to know something about the Bible. Whether a person is a believer or not, the Bible stands at the foundation of our form of civilization." What many people oppose, including those against the current Bible course in Odessa schools, is promoting one religion. As fifteen-year-old student Isla Moreno says, "I don't see a problem with them teaching a Bible class, but why teach a certain religion? There's kids who go to school with different religions." Moreno, who is Catholic, is one resident among many practicing diverse religions. Making sure that any course on the Bible in public schools does not promote a particular religion is a concern echoed by many residents.

When Southern Methodist University biblical scholar Mark A. Chancy reviewed the course, he found it to be primarily devotional. This is what worries many parents, including Amado Flore, an Odessa native and party to the lawsuit. He states "It's fine if kids want to get together to study the Bible. I'm all for that. What I'm not for is using tax dollars and public school resources to push an agenda."

Some residents defend the Christian angle to the study of the Bible based on American history. Permian High School senior Kelly Combs says, "It seems to me that if kids have an interest in anything, they should have the opportunity to be exposed to that. Our ancestors came to America to have Christian religious freedom." Because Odessa is a town whose population is primarily Christian, many residents feel the same way. Because the course is optional, many residents feel they should have the option to have the Bible course they want. Not all residents see it that way, though.

Odessa resident, parent, and teacher Lisa Roth, wrote a letter to the local newspaper in which she expressed her concerns about this issue, especially as a member of the Jewish community in the primarily Protestant town. "I object to a Bible class in public school that suggests the supremacy of one religion over another. You might think one religion IS better than another, but public school is not the place to teach this." Roth rejects the argument that because the course is an elective, she should not be concerned. "Just because it's an elective doesn't mean it won't affect my child or others. If we offered an elective promoting white supremacy, it would certainly have an effect on all students, whether they took the class or not." Her concern is that those students that are members of religious minorities will suffer even more ostracism if the Bible course is allowed to continue in a manner that endorses and promotes Protestantism over other religions.

The issue of whether or not to have a Bible class in public schools illustrates the tension inherent in the freedom of religion. On the one hand, freedom of religion means that an individual is free to engage in religious practices of their choosing. On the other hand, freedom of religion means that the same individual is free from government establishment of a particular religion. Deciding how much value to put on each is what gives people different opinions on policies about religion in public schools, such as whether to study the Bible, teach intelligent design, or allow prayer. *Introducing Issues with Opposing Viewpoints: Religion in Schools* explores how different people approach these debates and offers readers a look at the challenges faced by the issue of religion in public schools.

Chapter 1

Should Religion Be Allowed in Public Schools?

Students in an American Government class at Nathan Hale High School in Seattle discuss whether a law intended to stop harassment in the schools could have the consequence of preventing classroom discussion of religion, race, or other controversial topics.

Schools Should Be Neutral Toward Religion

Americans United for the Separation of Church and State

"In a multi-faith, religiously diverse society such as ours, neutrality is the appropriate stance for the government to take toward religion."

In this viewpoint, Americans United for Separation of Church and State takes the stand that government, including public schools, ought to stay out of the private religious lives of students. The organization clarifies this position with respect to school prayer and Bible study, refuting certain understandings of the Supreme Court's stance on the issue that would be hostile toward religion, prayer, and Bible study. The author endorses the stance of neutrality toward religion. Americans United for Separation of Church and State is a non-profit educational organization, founded in 1947 by a broad coalition of religious, educational, and civic leaders.

AS YOU READ, CONSIDER THE FOLLOWING QUESTIONS:

1. What did the Supreme Court rule regarding student prayer in public schools, as cited by the author?

2. What does the author report the Supreme Court ruled regarding Bible study in public schools?
3. According to the author, does neutrality toward religion mean being against religion?

Few issues in American public life engender more controversy than religion and public education. Unfortunately, this topic is all too often shrouded in confusion and misinformation. When discussing this matter, it's important to keep in mind some basic facts.

Ninety percent of America's youngsters attend public schools. These students come from homes that espouse a variety of religious and philosophical beliefs. Given the incredible diversity of American society, it's important that our public schools respect the beliefs of everyone and protect parental rights. The schools can best do this by not sponsoring religious worship. This principle ensures that America's public schools are welcoming to all children and leaves decisions about religion where they belong—with the family.

The U.S. Supreme Court has been vigilant in forbidding public schools—and other agencies of the government—to interfere with Americans' constitutional right to follow their own consciences when it comes to religion. In 1962, the justices ruled that official prayer had no place in public education.

Students Can Pray

This decision is widely misunderstood today. The court *did not* rule that students are forbidden to pray on their own; the justices merely said that government officials had no business composing a prayer for students to recite. The *Engel v. Vitale* case came about because parents in New York challenged a prayer written by a New York education board. These Christian, Jewish and Unitarian parents did not want their children subjected to state-sponsored devotions. The high court agreed that the scheme amounted to government promotion of religion.

In the following year, 1963, the Supreme Court handed down another important ruling dealing with prayer in public schools. In *Abington Township School District v. Schempp*, the court declared

Students and a Bible Club coach at Dover High School in Pennsylvania gather and pray by the school flagpole before the start of the school day, to celebrate a national day of prayer on Sept. 18, 2002.

school-sponsored Bible reading and recitation of the Lord's Prayer unconstitutional.

Since those rulings, a myth has sprung up asserting that Madalyn Murray O'Hair, a prominent atheist, "removed prayer from public schools." In fact, the 1962 case was brought by a group of New York parents who had no connection to O'Hair, and the 1963 case was filed by a Unitarian family from the Philadelphia area. O'Hair, at that time a resident of Baltimore, had filed a similar lawsuit, which the high court consolidated with the Pennsylvania case.

It is important to remember that in these decisions the Supreme Court did not "remove prayer from public schools." The court removed only *government-sponsored* worship. Public school students have always had the right to pray on their own as class schedules permit.

Also, the Supreme Court did not rule against official prayer and Bible reading in public schools out of hostility to religion. Rather, the justices held that these practices were examples of unconstitutional government interference with religion. Thus, the exercises violated the First Amendment.

Nothing in the 1962 or 1963 rulings makes it unlawful for public school students to pray or read the Bible (or any other religious book) on a voluntary basis during their free time. Later decisions have made this even clearer. In 1990, the high court ruled that high school students may form clubs that meet during "non-instructional" time to pray, read religious texts or discuss religious topics if other student groups are allowed to meet.

Religion Can Be Studied

The high court has also made it clear, time and time again, that objective study *about* religion in public schools is legal and appropriate. Many public schools offer courses in comparative religion, the Bible as literature or the role of religion in world and U.S. history. As long as the approach is objective, balanced and non-devotional, these classes present no constitutional problem.

In short, a public school's approach to religion must have a legitimate educational purpose, not a devotional one. Public schools should not be in the business of preaching to students or trying to persuade them to adopt certain religious beliefs. Parents, not school officials, are responsible for overseeing a young person's religious upbringing. This is not a controversial principle. In fact, most parents would demand these basic rights.

A passage from the high court's ruling in the 1963 Pennsylvania case sums up the proper role of religion in public education.

Justice Tom Clark, writing for the court, observed, "Nothing that we have said here indicates that such study of the Bible or of religion, when presented objectively as part of a secular program of education, may not be effected consistently with the First Amendment." Clark added that government could not force the exclusion of religion in schools "in the sense of affirmatively opposing or showing hostility to religion,"

The court's ruling suggested simply that a student's family, not government, is responsible for decisions about religious instruction and guidance. There was respect, not hostility, toward religion in the court's ruling.

Justice Clark concluded, "The place of religion in our society is an exalted one, achieved through a long tradition of reliance on the home, the church, and the inviolable citadel of the individual heart

and mind. We have come to recognize through bitter experience
that it is not within the power of
government to invade that citadel,
whether its purpose or effect be
to aid or oppose, to advance or
retard. In the relationship between
man and religion, the State is
firmly committed to a position of
neutrality."

Some critics of the high court's
rulings have suggested that these
church-state rulings have no precedence in American history. On the
contrary, the decisions are the logical outcome of a debate that has
been under way in our country for many decades.

History of Religion in Schools

Public education for the masses, as conceived by Horace Mann and
others in the mid 19th century, was intended to be "non-sectarian." In
reality, however, schools often reflected the majority religious view—a
kind of nondenominational Protestantism. Classes began with devotional readings from the King James Version of the Bible and recitation
of the Protestant version of the Lord's Prayer. Students were expected
to take part whether they shared those religious sentiments or not.

Catholic families were among the first to challenge these school-
sponsored religious practices. In some parts of the country, tension over
religion in public schools erupted into actual violence. In Philadelphia,
for example, full-scale riots and bloodshed resulted in 1844 over which
version of the Bible should be used in classroom devotions. Several
Catholic churches and a convent were burned; many people died. In
Cincinnati, a "Bible War" divided the city in 1868 after the school
board discontinued mandatory Bible instruction.

Tensions like this led to the first round of legal challenges to school-
sponsored religious activity in the late 19th century. Several states
ruled against the practices. Compelling children to recite prayers or
read devotionals from certain versions of the Bible, these courts said,
was not the job of public schools. They declared government-imposed
religion a violation of state constitutions and the fundamental rights

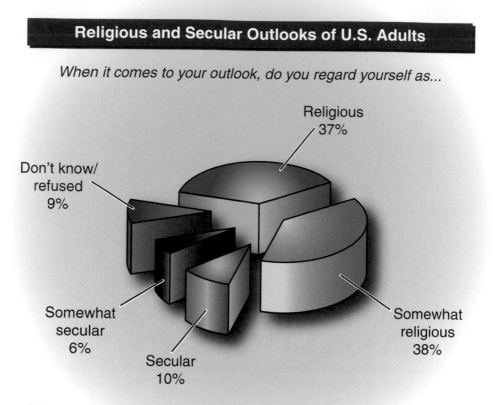

When it comes to your outlook, do you regard yourself as...

Religious
37%

Don't know/
refused
9%

Somewhat
secular
6%

Secular
10%

Somewhat
religious
38%

Taken from: Barry A. Kosmin, Seymour P. Lachman, et. Al., *American Religious Identity Survey*

of conscience. Eventually, the U.S. Supreme Court adopted this view as well, applying the church-state separation provisions of the First Amendment of the U.S. Constitution.

The Guidelines

The high court's decisions have worked well in practice. In 1995, a joint statement of current law regarding religion in public schools was published by a variety of religious and civil liberties organizations. This statement served as the basis for U.S. Department of Education guidelines intended to alleviate concerns about constitutional religious activities in schools.

These guidelines, which were sent to every public school in the nation, stressed that students have the right to pray or to discuss their religious views with their peers so long as they are not disruptive. But the guidelines went on to state that public schools are prohibited from sponsoring worship or pressuring students to pray, meditate, read religious texts or take part in other religious activities.

These are common-sense guidelines, but they are not enough for some people. Misguided individuals and powerful sectarian lobbies in Washington continue to press for religious majority rule in the nation's public schools. They advocate for school prayer amendments and other measures that would permit government-sponsored worship in the schools. They want their beliefs taught in the public schools and hope to use the public schools as instruments of evangelism.

In Favor of Neutrality

Americans must resist these efforts. They must protect the religious neutrality of public education. Being neutral on religion is not the same as being hostile toward it. In a multi-faith, religiously diverse society such as ours, neutrality is the appropriate stance for the government to take toward religion. Under this principle, public schools can allow for individual student religious expression without endorsing or promoting any specific faith.

The United States has changed since its founding in 1787. A nation that was once religiously homogeneous has become one of the most pluralistic and diverse on the face of the globe. Scholars count over 2,000 different denominations and traditions in our country.

The answer to disputes over religion in public schools is simple: Keep the government out of the private religious lives of students. Leave decisions about when and how to pray (or whether to pray at all) to the home. This is the course the Supreme Court has adopted, and we are a stronger nation for it.

As Supreme Court Justice Anthony Kennedy said in a June 1992 opinion, "No holding of this Court suggests that a school can persuade or compel a student to participate in a religious exercise. . . . The First Amendment's Religion Clauses mean that religious beliefs and religious expressions are too precious to be either proscribed or prescribed by the State."

The Absence of Religion Is Not Neutral Toward Religion

"Part of the frustration of some religious believers in this country is that they feel excluded by a public square where unbelief is the only belief system that is acceptable."

Brian P. Brennan

In the following viewpoint, Brian P. Brennan argues that atheism is its own belief system, just like any religion. As such, the author claims that the U.S. policy of having no religion in public schools has the effect of elevating atheism above other belief systems. Brennan argues that the religious education framework in Great Britain that includes both atheist belief systems and religious ones offers a more balanced approach to religious belief.

Brian P. Brennan is a graduate student in politics at St. Antony's College, Oxford University, England. He was a 2003 Pew Charitable Trusts Civitas Fellow in Faith and Public Affairs.

Brian P. Brennan, "Atheism Is Its Own Belief System," *National Catholic Reporter*, vol. 41, March 25, 2005, p. 15. Copyright © The National Catholic Reporter Publishing Company, 115 E. Armour Blvd., Kansas City, MO 64111. All rights reserved. Reproduced by permission of *National Catholic Reporter*, www.natcath.org.

AS YOU READ, CONSIDER THE FOLLOWING QUESTIONS:
1. What part of the new framework for religious education in Great Britain does the author discuss?
2. According to Brennan, how is religious education different in Great Britain from the United States?
3. What does the author think that the new framework in Great Britain does to atheism?

The curious relationship between church and state in Great Britain took a little-noted shift [in 2004] with the release of a new "national framework" for religious education in British schools. Largely drowned out in the babel leading up to the U.S. elections, the British government for the first time recognized atheism in the new framework as a belief system that should be taught alongside "traditional" faiths to British schoolchildren.

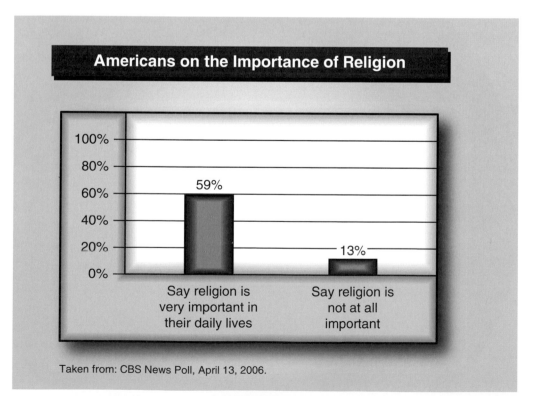

Americans on the Importance of Religion

59%

13%

Say religion is very important in their daily lives

Say religion is not at all important

Taken from: CBS News Poll, April 13, 2006.

Teaching Atheism and Religion

To the American observer, the response from religious leaders might seem remarkably tepid. Rather than protesting what might seem to be an elevation of atheism, the Church of England, the Muslim Council of Britain and the Catholic Bishops' Conference of England and Wales all issued statements welcoming the new framework. Indeed, it was the National Secular Society that complained that the new framework did not go far enough in allowing children to question religion.

If law permitted such education frameworks in the United States, it is easy to imagine some segments of America's churchgoing public spilling out into the streets to protest such a move. As it is, a first inclination may be to shake our heads at secularism's muscle in Europe. Yet given another look, the Brits' new education framework is not one that the religiously minded should be so quick to bemoan.

Differences Between Britain and America

Religious life in the United States and Great Britain may seem to have little in common. Religious education has always been a part of British education. National legislation mandates that such religious education programs "reflect the fact that religious traditions in Great Britain are mainly Christian, whilst taking account of the teaching and practices of the other principal religions represented in Great Britain." All the while, nary a week goes by without a church closing in the United Kingdom. The reasons for the dwindling numbers of Europeans who take their faith seriously depend on whom you ask. Some attribute it to a creeping relativism in European Protestantism, which, they say, has robbed it of its credibility. Others point to the overlap between church and state that, if it does not stain the church with politics as it once did, at least sucks the life out of faith.

For many American church leaders, the takeaway message of

> ## FAST FACT
>
> According to a survey, 77 percent of the U.S. population identify themselves as Christian; 14 percent are nonreligious, agnostic, or atheist; with the remaining 9 percent identifying with other religions such as Judaism, Islam, and Buddhism.

contemporary Christianity in Western Europe is "Don't let this happen to you." In the United States, mega-churches are popping up as fast as the exurbs can creep. We fumble for excuses about having God on our money, but have pretty well reined in prayer in the schoolhouse. Our guns are likely be pried from cold, dead hands before we will talk about setting standards for religious education in public schools. Hence whether you welcome the British decision or condemn it, it might seem irrelevant to the United States. Yet the fundamental question faced by those who developed the new British framework is one

Don Riley of Searcy, Arkansas, outside a Tangipahoa Parish School Board meeting in Amite, Louisiana, April 5, 2005. He is one of several people who prayed on the steps outside the meeting in a show of support for the board's fight to continue having prayers during board meetings.

that most of us in the United States have been assiduously avoiding for some time, and would do well to take on: When we are talking about the place of religion in the public square, just how comparable are atheism and "religion"?

Religion in Public Life

Americans have never been quite sure what part religion should play in public life. On the one hand, decisions about public policy are often predicated on our deepest held beliefs. On the other, in a pluralistic society, we cannot justify our policy prescriptions by pointing to a holy book, and expect everyone to be convinced. Should a senator get up on the floor and maintain that she voted for welfare reform because she felt a calling from God? Should a Congressional representative cast a vote for an amendment banning gay marriage because it is "against God's law"—and say as much? Are these appropriate arguments, even if one thinks they narrow the debate and exclude the unbeliever?

In recent decades, atheism has tried to hold itself above this fray. Some of its adherents have condemned "sectarian" argumentation, implying that believing in nothing is qualitatively different from believing in something. Part of the frustration of some religious believers in this country is that they feel excluded by a public square where unbelief is the only belief system that is acceptable. Yet in fact, atheism is the affirmative belief that there is no deity. If one follows [French philosopher Blaise] Pascal's famous wager, it may take more faith to affirm the absence of God than to maintain a belief in God's presence.

So is atheism properly considered a "belief system"? The British have said yes. While from the viewpoint of the religious partisan, the Brits' new education framework may appear to be the elevation of atheism, in fact it drags atheism down from the pedestal of public neutrality to which it has clung with white knuckles in recent years. Negotiating a place for belief in the public life of a pluralistic community—a place that serves to draw people in rather than driving them away—will always be difficult. Yet the British decision constitutes an important step in the process of reinvigorating the discussion. Rather than ceding the public square to those who consider themselves neutral because they are secular, we should allow ourselves to be provoked by our neighbors across the Atlantic.

The concerns and lively debate about the role of religious believers in American politics today is altogether fitting and needed. Yet we should not lose sight of the fact that those who see the world through the prism of disbelief are looking through a prism nonetheless and are not as different from their "religious" compatriots as they might think.

EVALUATING THE AUTHOR'S ARGUMENTS:

In this viewpoint, the author argued that the United States could learn something from Great Britain's stance toward religious education. Rather than being neutral toward religion, the author believes that the absence of religion in schools elevates the position of atheism. How do you think that the Americans United for the Separation of Church and State would answer his charge? Cite from the viewpoints in your answer.

Schools Should Accommodate Diverse Religious Needs

Charles Haynes

"In the current climate of anti-Muslim rhetoric, how schools . . . respond to the growth of Islam in this country is a real test of our national character."

In the following viewpoint, Charles Haynes discusses the issue of the accommodation of students' religious needs in public schools. Muslim students in particular need to pray several times a day and at length on Fridays. Haynes notes that while many students' religious needs do not need accommodation because they fall outside of regular school hours, Muslim students' needs pose a special challenge. The author calls on school districts to find a solution that can accommodate Muslim students without violating requirements to not encourage religious participation.

Charles Haynes is senior scholar and director of education programs at the First Amendment Center. He is also the author or coauthor of six books, including *The First Amendment in Schools* and *Finding Common Ground: A Guide to Religious Liberty in Public Schools.*

Charles Haynes, "Religious Liberty in Public Schools," *First Amendment Center,* Reproduced by permission.

AS YOU READ, CONSIDER THE FOLLOWING QUESTIONS:
1. What are some of the special religious needs that Muslim students have, according to Haynes?
2. According to the author, what kind of student prayer is currently allowed by the Constitution?
3. In what way are the needs of Muslim students different from Christian or Jewish students, in Haynes's opinion?

How far can public schools go in accommodating the religious needs of Muslim students? This question is presenting itself with increasing urgency, and it's a delicate balance to avoid doing too little or too much.

It isn't easy being a Muslim in America these days. The statistics are chilling. [In 2006] anti-Muslim violence, discrimination and harassment in the United States increased by nearly 70%, according to a report released [in April 2007] by the Council on American-Islamic Relations [CAIR]. (That's 1,019 incidents, CAIR said.).

The Religious Needs of Muslim Students

That's why Muslim students in public schools are often reluctant to ask school officials for accommodation for required prayers or other religious needs. But some things can't wait. When required daily prayers fall within the school day, for example, Muslim students need a place to pray. And when Muslim girls wearing head scarves arrive at a school with a "no head coverings" policy, they need an exemption on grounds of conscience.

Some school officials take a hard line—as when the Muskogee, Okla., school district suspended a Muslim girl for refusing to remove her scarf. Fortunately, most educators instinctively do the right thing and accommodate these requests. Even when they may not have to do so, they want to find some way to allow students to follow the requirements of their faith.

FAST FACT

According to a 2005 study by Encyclopaedia Britannica, there are 4,745,200 Muslims in the United States, which is 1.6 percent of the population.

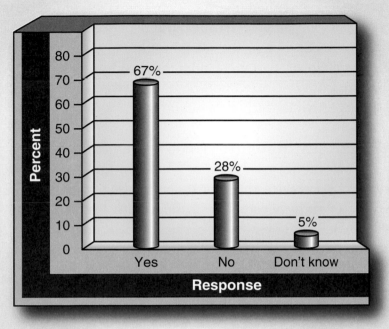

Americans' Perceptions: Is the U.S. a Christian Nation?

Taken from: The Pew Forum on Religion and Public Life Survey, 2006,
"*Many Americans Uneasy with Mix of Religion and Politics.*"

But there are limits to accommodation. Until recently, well-meaning administrators in two school districts (California and Texas) allowed Muslim students to use an empty classroom every Friday for congregational prayer, called Jum'ah. Given the complexities of student schedules, this arrangement meant that many students were released from class to join the hour-long gathering.

School officials have now put a stop to the practice in both places—not out of animus toward Islam, but because they realized they had crossed a First Amendment line.

Religious Rights at School

It's true that students in a public school are free to pray—alone or in groups—as long as they aren't disruptive and don't interfere with others' rights. If students want to pray between classes or at lunch in informal settings such as hallways or the cafeteria, they are free to do so. And there's no problem with allowing students to use a section of the library or a free classroom for brief prayers, as long as safety and discipline are maintained—and students don't miss much class.

But if schools get involved in releasing students from classes to attend a prayer service in the school building, that looks like a First Amendment violation to me. Under the establishment clause, administrators may not organize, sponsor, or otherwise entangle themselves in religious activities during the school day.

Meeting Every Students Needs

This is a painful line to draw. For Muslims, Jum'ah prayer isn't just another prayer service that can be performed at any time—it's an obligation of faith that must be fulfilled each Friday. Christians and Jews don't face this dilemma since the school calendar accommodates people with worship services on Saturday and Sunday (although some

Dave Gordon, the superintendant of schools for the Elk Grove Unified School District, announcing that the district will appeal a federal court ruling that the school cannot require children to recite the Pledge of Allegiance because it contains the words "under God."

Jews and Seventh-day Adventists are frozen out of the many school activities planned for Friday night and Saturday).

Rather than just saying "no," school districts have two other alternatives. If the secondary school allows extracurricular clubs, then Muslim students may form a student-led club under the Equal Access Act. They could meet for Jum'ah prayers every Friday if, and only if, all other extracurricular clubs are allowed to meet during that time. Given the academic program, rolling lunch periods and other scheduling problems, setting aside a "club period" on Friday may not be practical or possible for many schools. But it's one option.

Or schools could set up a released-time program on Fridays, allowing students to go off-campus for religious activities. Although school districts don't have to allow released-time, the Supreme Court has made clear that they may do so to meet needs of religious students and parents. School officials may not encourage or discourage participation, and they must allow all religious groups to participate.

As some school districts have discovered, releasing kids for an hour on Friday afternoon can be a problem. It's hard to get them back to finish the school day. But the burden of ensuring that students get to the worship service and back safely and on time is squarely on the religious community. If the local mosque (or church or synagogue) isn't willing to make this happen, then the program won't work.

Whatever the approach, school districts have a civic duty to look for a solution. In the current climate of anti-Muslim rhetoric, how schools—and all sectors of American society—respond to the growth of Islam in this country is a real test of our national character.

EVALUATING THE AUTHOR'S ARGUMENTS:

In this viewpoint, the author offers two alternatives that would allow Muslim students to fulfill their Friday religious obligations. Do you think either of these is a good solution? Why or why not?

Schools Should Not Accommodate Every Religious Need

Andy MacDonald

> "Public schools are government institutions, and as such they must be neutral in matters of religion."

In this viewpoint, Andy MacDonald argues that public schools need to be neutral on matters of religion. He argues that to remain neutral on religion, schools may not set aside classrooms for Muslim prayers during the school day. To do so, he argues, would constitute an establishment of religion and be in direct conflict with the U.S. Constitution. MacDonald believes that parents need to understand the secular nature of public schools and recognize that they do have the option to send their children to religious schools if public schools do not accommodate their religious beliefs.

Andy Macdonald, "Washington Schools Participate in Establishment of Religion," *SoundPolitics.com,* June 15, 2006. Reproduced by permission.

AS YOU READ, CONSIDER THE FOLLOWING QUESTIONS:
1. According to the author, what sorts of public school policies need to be neutral in matters of religion?
2. Does setting aside an empty classroom for Muslim students' prayer on Fridays violate the First Amendment prevention of establishment of religion, according to MacDonald?
3. According to the author, should public schools accommodate all religious needs of students as identified by their parents?

Public schools are government institutions, and as such they must be neutral in matters of religion. When they craft policies, such as determining when children must be in school,

Xavier Roberts and other children recite the Pledge of Allegiance in their third-grade classroom in California's Elk Grove Unified School District, March 3, 2003. Days later, a federal court upheld an earlier ruling that the school could not require students to say the Pledge as it contains the words "under God."

how many absences children are allowed, and under what circumstances parents may excuse an absence, those policies must not be tailored to any particular religion. Ideally, they should not mention religion at all—the same rule that allows an excused absence for Good Friday should allow one for visiting the Seattle Art Museum.

The typical response to having a neutral policy on prayer is: "Islam is unique. Practicing Muslims must pray five times a day, sometimes during school hours, and they should make those prayers in a mosque on Fridays." That is true, but it does not trump the First Amendment prevention of an establishment of religion or the Fourteenth Amendment guarantee of equal protection under the law. When a public education and the freedom of religion conflict, public education must give way. School administrators should keep this in mind when formulating education policy, in particular when making accommodations for religion.

Public and Private Schools

Percentage distribution of students in grades 1–12, by type of school; 1993 and 2003

Type of School	1993	2003
Public, assigned	79.9	73.9
Public, chosen	11.0	15.4
Private, church-related	7.5	8.4
Private, not church-related	1.6	2.4

Taken from: U.S. Department of Education, National Center for Education Statistics, 2006.

Establishment of Religion

An accommodation that seems common in public schools . . . is the practice of setting aside an empty classroom for Muslim prayer. This strikes me as an establishment of religion. Other students pray on campus, and some groups use school facilities for prayer when classes are not in session, but this seems to be the only instance where a religion may practice officially during the school day. As such, it puts the followers of Islam in a privileged position, and may reasonably lead students to conclude practicing Islam is ok with the school, but practicing another religion is not.

This is not to say that the school district should remain ignorant of the religious beliefs of its students. It should have an understanding of the teachings of the major religions and know the obligations each religion places on its adherents. It should do this not to create exceptional policies for believers, but rather so it can be better able to help parents understand the secular nature of the public schools. That way the parents can decide if a secular, government school is right for their children, or if another alternative better fits their religious beliefs.

EVALUATING THE AUTHOR'S ARGUMENTS:

In this viewpoint, Andy MacDonald argued that public schools should not accommodate Muslim students' Friday prayer needs. What do you think MacDonald would say about Charles Haynes's two alternatives for accommodation?

The Bible Should Be Taught in Public Schools

Rich Lowry

In the following viewpoint, Rich Lowry argues that the Bible should be taught as part of public school curriculum. The author claims that the Bible is part of American history. Furthermore, he claims that one cannot be educated without having Bible literacy because of the great number of biblical references in the works of numerous esteemed authors and because of the inspiration the Bible offered to numerous poets, painters and composers.

Rich Lowry is editor of the biweekly magazine *National Review* and author of *Legacy: Paying the Price for the Clinton Years.*

> *"America is a Bible-soaked nation."*

AS YOU READ, CONSIDER THE FOLLOWING QUESTIONS:

1. Why does the author say that "America is a Bible-soaked nation"?
2. Why does Lowry believe that you must have Bible education to be educated?
3. What percentage of public-school teenagers report that their school offers the Bible or religion as part of the curriculum, according to the author?

It's time to get the Bible back in public schools. And not through the back door of creationism disguised as Intelligent Design.

America is a Bible-soaked nation, from the Puritans to Abraham Lincoln to Martin Luther King Jr. Without a basic grasp of the Bible, it is impossible to understand the well springs of our country and the basis of Western civilization. Which is why it is a scandal that Bible education has been chased out of the schools and why the work of the Bible Literacy Project to put it back there is so admirable.

The nonpartisan, Virginia-based Bible Literacy Project has set out methodically to return Bible education to the schools by answering the questions: Is it legal? Is it needed? How can it be done? "The Bible and Its Influence," a just-published textbook for use in grades 9–12, is the culmination of this effort. Rarely is a textbook an occasion for celebration or anything but moaning on the part of students, but this substantial, gorgeously produced, thoroughly vetted volume is an emphatic exception.

A few years ago, the Bible Literacy Project published together with the First Amendment Center a guide on how to teach the Bible in schools. The list of groups that have endorsed this consensus statement reads like a who's who from the clashing sides in the culture war, with People For the American Way Foundation on the one hand and National Association of Evangelicals on the other. In 1963, the guide notes, the Supreme Court struck down devotional Bible reading in schools as unconstitutional. But the court said schools may teach the Bible as long as it is "presented objectively as part of a secular program of education"—a message lost on most lawsuit-averse school boards.

Is Bible Education Necessary?

So, Bible education is legal, but is it necessary? Well, only if you want to be educated. By one count, there are 1,300 biblical references in

John Waggoner presents a petition asking the Ector Independent School Board in Odessa, Texas, to institute an elective course on the Bible, April 26, 2005. The petition bore over 6,000 signatures, and after its presentation the school board voted to add the class to the high school curriculum.

Shakespeare's plays, working out to an average of 40 per play. Bible literacy will lead to a deeper understanding of authors from Herman Melville to Charles Dickens, from William Faulkner to Toni Morrison. The Bible has inspired the world's greatest poets, painters and composers, some of its most influential reformers, and the founding of a great nation (ours).

But only 8 percent of public-school teenagers report that their school offers the Bible or religion as part of the curriculum. A Gallup survey of high-school students found that large numbers know the very basics (Adam and Eve, etc.), but not much more. Two-thirds of teens couldn't correctly identify, given four options, a quotation from the Sermon on the Mount. They didn't know what happened on the road to Damascus. About ten percent think Moses was one of the Twelve Apostles.

As a Bible Literacy Project report put it, "No other book of comparable influence and importance could be deliberately excluded from public-school curricula without drawing sharp criticism from the educational and scientific elites." Secularists love debates like that over Intelligent Design that supposedly pit religion against the dictates of sound education. Here is a debate that has long pitted Bible-fearing (in their own peculiar way) ACLU [American Civil Liberties Union]-types against the obvious educational imperative of familiarizing students with the most influential book of all time.

"The Bible and Its Influence," carefully crafted to be within legal parameters and approved by dozens of scholars from diverse religious backgrounds, takes away any excuse to shy away from Bible education. . . . It is Michael Newdow-proof.* Charles Haynes of the First Amendment Center has written, "At long last, here is an answer for beleaguered school districts that want to offer a Bible course, but don't want to get sued."

But inertia is a strong force, especially for overly cautious school hoards. Parents who think the Bible should be part of education need to tell their school systems about this new book. It is a way to return the Bible to schools, without lawsuits or sectarian rancor.

EVALUATING THE AUTHOR'S ARGUMENTS:

In this viewpoint, Rich Lowry claimed that students need Bible education in order to be educated. Do you agree? Why or why not?

---

* Michael Newdow sued the government over the inclusion of the phrase "under God" in the Pledge of Allegiance.

Viewpoint

6

The Bible Should Not Be Taught in Public Schools

Jim West

"Using any religious text as teaching material in publicly funded educational institutions is not proper."

In the following viewpoint, Jim West argues that the Bible should not be taught in public schools. West has two main concerns about this issue. He is concerned about problems with determining who will teach the Bible, and he is concerned about the problems that will arise in determining how the Bible will be taught. Since every student is not Christian and every Christian is not alike in understanding the Bible, West is concerned that there will be no way to develop the course in a way that does not run into the problem of education crossing the line into indoctrination.

Jim West is pastor of Petros Baptist Church in Petros, Tennessee.

AS YOU READ, CONSIDER THE FOLLOWING QUESTIONS:

1. What is the author's concern about qualifications to teach the Bible?
2. What is West's worry about sectarian viewpoints?
3. What is the author's concern about source materials?

Texas state representative Warren Chisum. In April 2007, Chisum introduced a bill to the Texas legislature that would require all high schools in the state to offer a class on the Bible.

Terry Redmon is an activist trying to persuade the school board of Wilson County, Tennessee, to implement a "Bible elective" course to help students understand the Book's impact on world history.

At face value this would seem to be remarkably important, especially from the point of view of a devout Christian like Redmon, who insists he isn't out to convert students but only to educate them.

Look closer, however, and one finds problems associated with the phenomenon of public-school Bible courses.

Who Should Teach?

First, are those who are slated to teach such courses qualified to do so? If a teacher in secondary or elementary school teaches math, they are required to possess a certificate in that subject. History is the same, and so is science.

In other words, teachers have to be qualified to teach their subject matter. What qualification requirements will be in place for the courses Redmon is suggesting? Will those teaching the Bible elective have sufficient background in the subject to do it justice, or will they be out of their element and misinform their students?

Another problem is akin to the first. Are Catholics competent to teach Baptists about the Bible? Will Mormons, Jehovah's Witnesses or Jews be asked to teach the children of Methodists and Presbyterians and Episcopalians?

Where the Bible is concerned, sectarian viewpoints are inextricably involved. What are mother and father devout Southern Baptist going to think when little Billy comes home from school and tells them his Bible teacher at school is a Muslim?

Problems will erupt over who is chosen to teach the course. Who will make that choice? What will the qualifications be? Is the school board equipped to evaluate whether a choice is proper?

How Will It Be Taught?

A third problem centers on what source materials will the teachers be using. Redmon appears to be insisting on one created by North Carolina–based National Council on the Bible Curriculum in Public Schools. Favored by the Religious Right, this material has been shown to be utterly inadequate and quite skewed in the direction of very conservative thinkers. Other curricula are available, of course, but no matter what curriculum is chosen, it will have its detractors.

This means that problems will naturally arise between those desirous of adopting one curriculum and those desirous of another, simply adding logs to the fire of an already contentious issue.

Further, is the . . . school board . . . comprised of trained biblical scholars, theologians, and exegetes who know the issues at hand and are therefore capable of evaluating suggested materials?

Another problem may not occur to many who live in the Bible Belt,

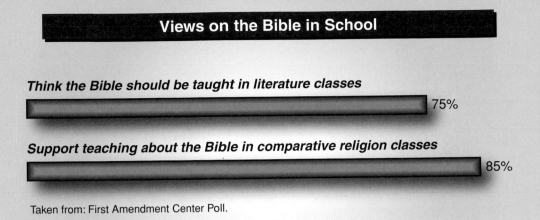

but in other parts of the country it will add still more discomfort. And that is everyone is not Christian.

Put the shoe on the other foot. Imagine your Christian son or daughter is attending a school in a large city where the dominant religion is Islam. In school each day the teacher reads from the Quran and students are expected to read it, study it, familiarize themselves with it and master its contents.

As a devoted Christian, will this seem more like "education" or "indoctrination?" For this reason alone, using any religious text as teaching material in publicly funded educational institutions is not proper.

There are a number of problems with "Bible elective" courses: Will the teachers teaching them be qualified? Will they allow their own religious perspective to inform their handling of the biblical text? Will the base materials be high quality or sectarian, biased and skewed? And what of all those of other faith traditions who will rightly, and should rightly, request that their own sacred texts be also taught as elective subjects? Will they be allowed the same respect, the same dignity and the same equality?

Or is the "Bible elective" movement simply a thinly disguised attempt to foist upon society a particular and particularistic theocratic vision where the Bible eventually replaces scientific and literary texts and historical sourcebooks to become the only material taught and learned?

Are our uncertain times, societal fears and dread of terror subconsciously driving us back to the 19th century, to splendid isolationism, to one-room school houses where the Bible is the only textbook and knowing it is seen as equivalent to knowing all things important? It's hard to tell.

EVALUATING THE AUTHOR'S ARGUMENTS:

In this viewpoint, Jim West asked the reader to imagine being a Christian parent of public-school children in a predominantly Muslim city where there is a course on the Quran. What is the author's point in asking the reader to imagine this? What do you think Rich Lowry would say to West in response?

Chapter 2

Should Public Schools Teach Intelligent Design?

Attorney and Intelligent Design advocate Richard Thompson on his way into a Harrisburg, Pennsylvania, courtroom on Sept. 28, 2005. Thompson is defending the Dover Area School District's requirement that Intelligent Design be taught in biology classes.

Viewpoint

1

Intelligent Design Should Be Taught as an Alternative to Darwinian Evolution

Stafford Betty

"Intelligent design theory is not based on the Bible or any other scripture."

In the following viewpoint, Stafford Betty argues that the theory of intelligent design should be taught in public schools. Betty claims that the theory of intelligent design is perfectly compatible with a belief in evolution, but not with Darwinian evolution. Betty defends the theory of intelligent design from the charge that it is unscientific. He believes that the theory of intelligent design is good science while the theory of Darwinian evolution is not good science. As such, he endorses the view that intelligent design should be taught in the science classrooms of public schools.

Stafford Betty is professor of religious studies at California State University–Bakersfield.

Dr. Stafford Betty, "Intelligent Design Theory Belongs in the Science Classroom," *National Catholic Reporter*, vol. 42, October 21, 2005, p. 23. Copyright © The National Catholic Reporter Publishing Company, 115 E. Armour Blvd., Kansas City, MO 64111. All rights reserved. Reproduced by permission of National Catholic Reporter, www.natcath.org.

AS YOU READ, CONSIDER THE FOLLOWING QUESTIONS:
1. What is the difference between Darwinian evolution and the evolution that the author believes is fact?
2. Why does Betty think that the account of genetic accidents used to support Darwinian evolution does not succeed?
3. Does the author think that the theory of intelligent design is scientific or unscientific?

Although a frequent critic of President Bush, I think he was correct to say that intelligent design theory deserves a mention in science classrooms alongside Darwinian evolution.

Intelligent design theory is not based on the Bible or any other scripture. It is not creationism in disguise, as opponents of intelligent design misleadingly claim. Intelligent design accepts evolution as a fact. It accepts an ancient earth (4.6 billion years) and a still more ancient universe (13.7 billion years). It accepts all the findings of responsible science. But it does not accept Darwinism.

Darwinism is not the same thing as evolution. It is a particular theory of how evolution occurred. According to Darwinism, the entire process was unguided and happened "naturally." Intelligent design theorists contest this claim. They call into question Darwinian evolution's cardinal doctrine, natural selection. Proponents of natural selection claim that the process by which more complex organisms arise from less complex ones is not guided by any intelligence. Proponents of intelligent design say it is.

Supporters of intelligent design hold that Darwinian evolution is not good science. Here is why:

According to the tenets of Darwinian evolution, a genetic accident within a member of a species sometimes (actually rarely) has a beneficial effect on the species. Consider archaeopteryx, the transitional form between dinosaur and bird that Darwinian evolution holds is the ancestor of

FAST FACT

William Paley, born in 1743 in England, was a proponent of intelligent design who wrote *A View of the Evidence of Christianity*. Charles Darwin studied Paley's work, but ultimately rejected his argument.

birds as we know them. A long series of genetic accidents gradually turns the dinosaur's forearm into a feathery appendage (wing) that enables the archaeopteryx to better flee its enemy by soaring above the ground. And that advantage gives it a much better chance of surviving. Thus birds evolve from dinosaurs, according to standard Darwinian teaching. In a similar manner every species has evolved. All is explained by a long series of lucky genetic accidents, the survival of the fittest, and a steady march forward across hundreds of millions of years from blue-green algae to Mother Teresa.

Genetic Accidents

The theory sounds great, as no doubt you were told in your high school biology class. But it has one potentially fatal flaw. Let's get back to the example of the feathery appendage. There is no evidence that the wing evolved in one fell swoop. Darwinians grant that it took a whole series of genetic accidents spanning millions of years for the wing to fully evolve. At first there was just some extra fluff on the dinosaur's forearms. Then a little more. Then still more. Then something that resembled feathers. Then more feathers. And finally two wings that enabled the first proto-bird to rise off the ground.

Do you begin to see the problem? What survival advantage did the first genetic accident resulting in a little extra fluff on its forearms give the dinosaur? Or even the 20th fortuitous accident resulting in something genuinely feathery? None that intelligent design can see, because the dinosaur still can't fly. So what would push the dinosaur along such a line of evolutionary development? Nothing that intelligent design can see *unless there was some kind of intelligence guiding the evolution*. Some kind of intelligence that saw in advance that this long and gradual process would result in that marvelous life form we refer to as a bird. Some kind of intelligence that wanted birds inhabiting our earth and knew how to bring it about—by a *guided* evolution.

There are thousands of instances like this that resist explanation via Darwinian evolution. Try explaining, for example, what the survival value was for us when our ancestors lost their tails and fur. We find hairy apes at the equator and some of the least hairy humans on the planet inside the Arctic Circle. Natural selection? This is just one of many anomalies that leave me scratching my head and looking for some other explanation.

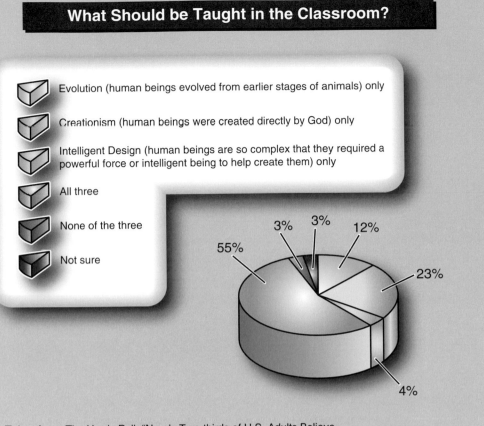

What Should be Taught in the Classroom?

Evolution (human beings evolved from earlier stages of animals) only

Creationism (human beings were created directly by God) only

Intelligent Design (human beings are so complex that they required a powerful force or intelligent being to help create them) only

All three

None of the three

Not sure

55%   3%   3%   12%   23%   4%

Taken from: The Harris Poll, "Nearly Two-thirds of U.S. Adults Believe Human Beings Were Created by God," July 6, 2005.

Scientific or Unscientific?

Opponents of intelligent design label this "other explanation" unscientific. Is it? Supporters of intelligent design claim that evolution was guided; supporters of Darwinian evolution claim it wasn't. Is it really unscientific to claim that an unseen intelligence guided the evolution? I don't see why. Human intelligence is unseen. But we all know that it's behind our homes and our cities. To acknowledge that in almost every case intelligent choices create order isn't unscientific.

Is it unscientific to point out the weakness in Darwinian evolution? Leading theorists of intelligent design such as Michael Behe and William Dembski think it's *good* science. They single out organs, like the human eye, or even highly complex molecules and show that they are "irreducibly complex"—that is, the supposed transitional forms

Students leaving the Dover Area High School in Dover, Pennsylvania, December 20, 2005. The school was at the center of a lawsuit over whether Intelligent Design could be taught as a scientific theory.

leading to but falling well short of them wouldn't have been any more fit to survive than their starting point. So how could the end product have evolved? Unless of course, it was all along on the radarscope of an unseen intelligence guiding the evolution to its target, as most Catholics believe.

The argument presented here is not based on the Bible. True, many Bible-based Christians have championed it. It is, after all, much more compatible with their beliefs than Darwinian evolution, for there is nothing to rule out the possibility that the unseen intelligence is much more than a designer. But what one's faith adds to the designer does not affect the validity of the argument for intelligent design.

I will conclude by quoting from Einstein. "You will hardly find one among the profounder sort of scientific minds without peculiar religious feeling of his own. . . . His religious feeling takes the form of a rapturous amazement at the harmony of natural law, which reveals an intelligence of such superiority that, compared with it, all the systematic thinking and acting of human beings is an utterly insignificant reflection."

The "intelligence" Einstein refers to is the same sort of intelligence intelligent design points to. Would anyone want to claim that Einstein's conclusions are unscientific or faith based or his reasoning invalid? Or that his views are inappropriate for a science classroom?

EVALUATING THE AUTHOR'S ARGUMENTS:

In this viewpoint, Stafford Betty argued that the theory of intelligent design is not based on the Bible and only proves the existence of an intelligent designer. Do you think that it is possible to teach the theory of intelligent design without endorsing any particular religious beliefs? Why or why not?

Intelligent Design Is Not a Competing Theory to Darwinian Evolution

Edward Humes

"Real evolution isn't random; it doesn't say man came from monkeys."

In the following viewpoint, Edward Humes argues that those who purport to show problems with the theory of evolution in order to support the theory of intelligent design mischaracterize the theory of evolution. Humes believes that there are two theories of evolution, and the one that is discounted by proponents of intelligent design is not the real theory but rather a "straw-man" image of the theory made easy to knock down. Humes claims that the theory of evolution is much more sophisticated and that intelligent design is not a competitor to this theory.

Edward Humes is the author of *Monkey Girl: Evolution, Education, Religion and the Battle for America's Soul.*

AS YOU READ, CONSIDER THE FOLLOWING QUESTIONS:
1. What are the "two theories of evolution" as cited by the author?
2. What is the "talk-radio version" of evolution, according to Humes?
3. What is the "real" theory of evolution, according to the author?

When I first arrived at the Ronald Reagan Federal Building and Courthouse in Harrisburg, Pa., for what was billed as the second coming of the Scopes "monkey trial," [a 1905 case concerning the teaching of evolution in school] a man mingling with the media gaggle handed me an invitation to a lecture titled "Why Evolution Is Stupid." The fellow advised me to come hear the truth about Charles Darwin's dangerous idea. Then he jerked a thumb toward the courtroom and said "You're sure not going to hear it in there."

Guillermo Gonzalez is an assistant professor of physics and astronomy at Iowa University and an outspoken proponent of intelligent design.

Two Theories of Evolution

I had gone to Harrisburg to research a book, expecting cutting-edge arguments for the theory of evolution pitted against an upstart movement called "intelligent design," which claims there is evidence of a master designer inside living cells. And hear them I did, in frequently riveting (and occasionally stupefying) detail, as the judge considered whether teaching intelligent design in public schools breached the wall separating church and state.

And yet that invitation and the angry, volatile town meeting it led me to proved even more enlightening. It showed me an essential truth of this nation's culture wars that seems especially relevant today [February 12, 2007], Darwin's 198th birthday: There are really two theories of evolution. There is the genuine scientific theory, and there is the talk-radio pretend version, designed not to enlighten but to deceive and enrage.

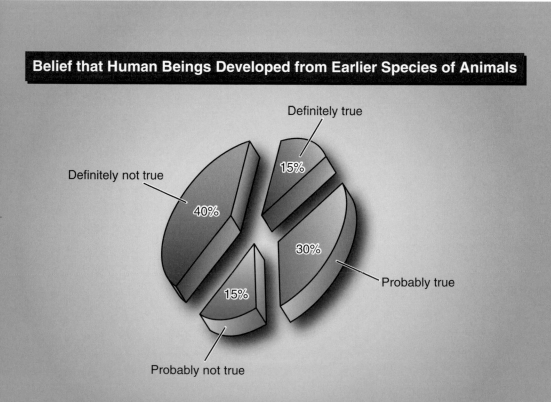

Belief that Human Beings Developed from Earlier Species of Animals

Definitely true
15%

Definitely not true
40%

30%
Probably true

15%

Probably not true

Taken from: Association of Religion Data Archives (ARDA), "General Social Survey," 2004.

The talk-radio version had a packed town hall up in arms at the "Why Evolution Is Stupid" lecture. In this version of the theory, scientists supposedly believe that all life is accidental, a random crash of molecules that magically produced flowers, horses and humans—a scenario as unlikely as a tornado in a junkyard assembling a 747. Humans come from monkeys in this theory, just popping into existence one day. The evidence against Darwin is overwhelming, the purveyors of talk-radio evolution rail, yet scientists embrace his ideas because they want to promote atheism.

These are just a few highlights of the awful and pervasive straw-man image of evolution that pundits harp about in books and editorials and, yes, on talk radio, and this cartoon version really is stupid. No wonder most Americans reject evolution in poll after poll.

The Real Theory

But then there is the real theory of evolution, the one that was on display in that Harrisburg courtroom, for which there is overwhelming evidence in labs, fossils, computer simulations and DNA studies. Most Americans have not heard of it. Teachers give it short shrift in schools because the subject upsets too many parents who only know the talk-radio version. But real evolution isn't random; it doesn't say man came from monkeys. Those claims are made up by critics to get people riled up—paving the way for pleasing alternatives like intelligent design.

Real evolutionary theory explains how life forms change across generations by passing on helpful traits to their offspring; a process that, after millions of years, gradually transforms one species into another. This does not happen randomly but through nature's tendency to reward the most successful organisms and to kill the rest.

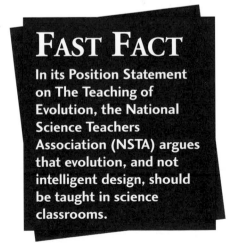

FAST FACT

In its Position Statement on The Teaching of Evolution, the National Science Teachers Association (NSTA) argues that evolution, and not intelligent design, should be taught in science classrooms.

This is why germs grow resistant to antibiotics and why some turtles are sea animals and others survive quite nicely in the desert, and why dinosaurs—and more than 99% of all other species that have ever lived on Earth—are extinct.

The environment changes. The recipe for survival changes with it. And life changes to keep up—or it dies. Darwin's signature insight is both brilliant and elegantly, brutally simple.

The real theory of evolution does not try to explain how life originated—that remains a mystery. The truth is that many scientists accept evolution *and* believe in God—and in a natural world so complete that it strives toward perfection all on its own, without need of a supernatural designer to keep it going.

The judge in Pennsylvania eventually found that real evolution was not stupid; that intelligent design was religion, not science, and that the school board in Dover, Pa., whose actions had precipitated this replay of Scopes, was out of line. Judge John E. Jones III was rewarded for his sensible and well-documented ruling with death threats. Such is the power of talk-radio evolution.

Meanwhile, a creationist history of the Grand Canyon is on sale in national park shops. A major American museum expressed interest in having me speak about my new book but decided the subject of evolution was too "political" right now to risk it. And teachers across the nation tell me they feel compelled to downplay or skip evolution lessons to avoid controversy; one L.A.-area high school instructor said she is the only one of five science teachers on her faculty to even mention evolution in class, notwithstanding a clear state mandate to teach it.

Judge Jones has since told me that his only regret in the case is that he did not bend the rules to allow live TV coverage so more people could see the powerful evidence supporting his decision. Because the one thing the prophets of talk-radio evolution have, it seems, is the loudest megaphone.

Viewpoint

3

Teaching Intelligent Design Can Increase Acceptance of Evolution

Michael Balter

"The best way to teach the theory of evolution is to teach [its] contentious history."

In the following viewpoint, Michael Balter discusses the differences between the way Great Britain and the United States approach the teaching of alternatives to evolution. Looking at the differences in the popularity of evolution compared with other theories in each country, he concludes that offering alternatives to evolution within the classroom actually has the effect of increasing the number of people who accept the theory of evolution. Balter argues that facing the contentious history of the theory of evolution in the classroom will result in more people's choosing evolution more often than if evolution is the only theory taught.

Michael Balter writes for the magazine *Science.*

In January, Britain's Qualifications and Curriculum Authority issued new guidelines for teaching about science and religion. They include some excellent ideas. For example, the guidelines encourage teachers to stage historical debates between science and religion, with students taking the roles of Charles Darwin, Galileo and even Richard Dawkins, the Oxford University scientist and outspoken atheist.

In another exercise, students are asked to write an essay on the following topic: "The world is very complex. Does this mean that it must have been the work of a creator God?"

These suggestions, which are designed for 14-year-old students, are intended only for religion classes, and not the science curriculum. That is a pity, because a confrontation between scientific and religious views of the universe would be an ideal way to teach science—especially a subject as contentious as the theory of evolution.

So far, however, British scientists and their supporters have managed to keep creationism out of the classroom, along with its latter-day incarnation, intelligent design (the "thinking man's creationism," as *Science* magazine put it recently).

Comparing Great Britain with the United States

In the United States, despite strong pressure from religious groups, a 1987 Supreme Court decision banning classroom teaching of creationism has held up.

Given the theory of evolution's monopoly in the classroom, one

> **FAST FACT**
>
> The theory of intelligent design is often studied in philosophy classes at the university level. The study of philosophy is not usually offered in primary or secondary school.

might think that it has gained a steady stream of converts over the years. But a poll taken for the BBC [British Broadcasting Corporation] found that the British public was split on the issue: Only 48 percent of respondents thought evolution best explained the development of life on earth, while 22 percent chose creationism, 17 percent intelligent design, and the rest said they did not know.

As depressing as those figures might be to scientists, they are pretty good compared to the results of similar surveys in the United States. A Gallup poll in November 2004 found that only 13 percent of respondents thought that God had no part in the evolution or creation of human beings, while 45 percent said they believed that God had created humans in their present form within the last 10,000 years or so.

To be sure, this chronic skepticism about evolutionary theory reflects the continuing strong influence of religion. Yet it also implies that scientists have not been persuasive enough, even when buttressed by strong scientific evidence that natural selection alone can account for life's complexity.

The Problem with Evolution's Monopoly

Could it be that the theory of evolution's monopoly in the classroom has backfired?

For one thing, this monopoly strengthens claims by creationists and intelligent-design proponents that scientists don't want to be challenged. More importantly, it shields Darwinian theory from challenges that, when properly refuted, might win over adherents to evolutionary views.

A few years ago, a biology instructor at a university in Washington State set out to test this idea.

First-year biology majors were divided into four sections. Two groups were assigned portions of Dawkins' "The Blind Watchmaker," a pro-evolution book, as well as a book advocating intelligent design called "Icons of Evolution." These groups also viewed a short animated creationist film and read an online rebuttal of creationist ideas, as well as materials on the nature and history of science. The other two groups read only evolutionary materials.

At the end of the course, the students were invited to take a voluntary, anonymous survey about possible changes in their outlooks. The

Roman Catholic Cardinal Schoenborn of Vienna, Austria, at a Feb. 7, 2007, meeting where he condemned the Kitzmiller v. Dover decision that banned the teaching of Intelligent Design in biology classes.

results, published in the November 2005 issue of the journal *BioScience*, found that 61 percent of students exposed to both creationism and evolution changed their outlooks, while only 21 percent of students exposed only to evolution did so—and nearly all of the changes were from the creationist to the evolutionist direction.

The instructor concluded that directly and respectfully engaging with students' beliefs, rather than ignoring them as most science teachers are forced to do, could be a more effective way to teach evolution.

Soon after this study was published. I got into a ferocious debate with commentators on a pro-evolution blog, who argued that this approach was all fine and dandy for university students but too advanced for high school students.

Yet the first-year students in Washington were just out of high school, and the new British guidance for religion classes—which uses a similar strategy—is aimed at 14-year-olds.

The polls show that scientists and science teachers have little to lose and everything to gain by bringing creationism into the classroom, where it can be critically debated and its merits compared to those of evolutionary theory.

Contentious History

The history of the theory is one of bitter debates between science and religion. In "On the Origin of Species," Darwin refuted the arguments for intelligent design put forward by the 18th century English philosopher William Paley, who had greatly influenced Darwin until he visited the Galapagos Islands and saw natural selection at work. Over the ensuing decades, Darwin's theories were rigorously tested and criticized before they won over even the majority of scientists.

The best way to teach the theory of evolution is to teach this contentious history. The most effective way to convince students that the theory is correct is to confront, not avoid, the continuing challenges to it.

EVALUATING THE AUTHOR'S ARGUMENTS:

In this viewpoint, Michael Balter argued that the best way to teach evolution is to discuss all the contentious alternatives, such as creationism and intelligent design. Do you think Humes, the author of the previous viewpoint, could accept Balter's conclusion? Why or why not?

Intelligent Design Cannot Be Tested Scientifically

Richard Fortey

"A worthwhile theory always suggests new lines of investigation, and on this criterion Darwinism has passed with flying colours."

In the following viewpoint, Richard Fortey argues that the theory of intelligent design is antithetical to the scientific process involving investigation and discovery. While the theory of evolution encourages research, the theory of intelligent design suppresses research by positing an explanation that cannot be tested, Fortey contends.

Richard Fortey is a senior paleontologist at the Natural History Museum in London and a Fellow of the Royal Society. He is the author of *Life: A Natural History of the First Four Billion Years of Life on Earth, Trilobite: Eyewitness to Evolution,* and *Earth: An Intimate History.*

AS YOU READ, CONSIDER THE FOLLOWING QUESTIONS:
1. According to Fortey, are there scientists who believe in creationism?

2. According to the author, can scientists refute the theory of intelligent design by experiment?
3. For scientists, how does the theory of evolution differ from the theory of intelligent design, according to Fortey?

Scientists have found themselves trapped into appearing to be unreasonable in their pursuit of rationality. A snare has been cleverly set by the proponents of Intelligent Design in their quest to prove that Charles Darwin got it wrong.

The vast majority of scientists feel nothing but distress that the teaching of Intelligent Design has been promoted in a number of our schools, particularly the faith schools apparently beloved by [then British prime minister] Tony Blair. Fundamentalists of both Islamic and Christian persuasion meet on this rather implausible common ground. Both these groups of religious hard liners deplore Darwin and all his works.

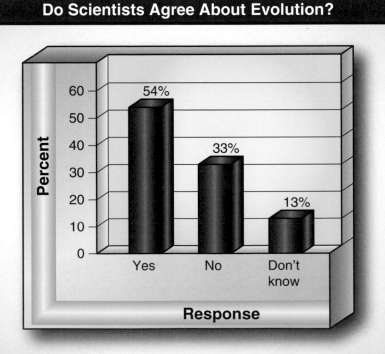

Do Scientists Agree About Evolution?

Taken from: The Pew Forum on Religion and Public Life Survey, 2005, "Public Divided on Origins of Life."

Scientists tend to get angry when confronted by what they see as the gross distortion of truth promulgated by Intelligent Designers. This has come across badly in 'balanced' debates in the media. As was the case with arguments over the MMR [Measles, mumps, and rubella] vaccine, the scientist when provoked can unwittingly appear to be a fulminating zealot. By contrast, many of the proponents of Intelligent Design (ID) have contrived to appear to be in favour of free speech. Aren't those scientists empurpled with rage and crying 'nonsense' the very picture of a threatened Establishment? On this platform the evolutionary scientist rather than the ID enthusiast can seem to be the less reasonable of the two.

Just a Theory

The trouble stems from the use of the weasel word "theory". Successive Presidents of the United States have got themselves off the hook with the influential Christian fundamentalist lobby by the deployment of this useful but traitorous word. Ronald Reagan would flash his aw-shucks smile and amiably reiterate: "I guess Evolution is just a theory". This has become a mantra among ID proponents. If evolution is one theory—then ID is another, or so the argument goes. Only a bigot would object to the airing of the alternative explanations.

The crux of ID is that evolution is purposeful, and that an 'invisible hand' has operated at crucial stages to direct the course of life onwards and upwards. The Intelligence of the Designer is manifest at certain critical points—such as the creation of life itself.

On the other hand, the scientific 'theory' of evolution actually breaks into two components. The first part is to assert that descent of all organisms from a common ancestor has, indeed, happened. To deny this is the equivalent of believing that the earth is flat as a pancake, or that the sun goes round it. Both could be described as theories, though nobody has taken them seriously for hundreds of years. Some fundamentalists still believe that creation happened a few thousand years ago. No respectable scientist believes this. Since the unscrambling of the genome has recently been added to evidence from the fossil record, it might be said that descent is simply a fact. We share genes with bananas and bacteria. At this deep level, DNA proves that humans are joined to all other life. This ought to awake nothing but wonder in all of us, but some find the thought of such a brotherhood of life scary.

The other part of Darwinism says that natural selection is the driving force behind evolution. This is where the ID protagonists come in. They accept the long time scale required from what we know of the age of the earth, but substitute supernaturally directed selection at critical points in life's long history. They might say that proteins are too darn complicated to have arisen by natural selection alone. This kind of assertion drives rationalists crazy, because it is impossible to refute by a critical experiment. There will always be another protein, another example of that supposed extra, guiding ingredient.

Intelligent Design Theory Suppresses Questions

The problem for scientists is that when this additional design factor is added it serves only to suppress questions—and science is all about tackling questions head-on. Why should we spend money on setting up experiments to simulate the creation of the first living cell if the motive force was a "designer"? No experiment can detect such metaphysical seasoning in the primeval soup.

Science has always been about tackling new areas of knowledge, with theory and experiment interacting creatively. If God's influence is invoked for any breakthrough in life's story, research is simply stopped dead in its tracks: no point in investigating further. ID therefore becomes a brake on discovery, not a way of enriching it.

In my view, God has overly got mixed into the argument. Scientists are often presented as the champions of atheism. This is typified by [revolutionary biologist and atheist] Richard Dawkins' views of theistic "delusion". Although I might agree with much of what Dawkins has to say, it might be that his almost theological espousal of atheism has served to up the stakes in the ID debate. In fact, there are many world-class scientists who are also believers. But they also believe that God should not be introduced into the explanation of nature. Scientists of my generation remember the meretricious [false] attractions of

Dr. Kenneth Miller of Brown University's Department of Molecular Biology speaking to the Ohio State Board of Education in 2002. Brown is a vocal critic of Intelligent Design, which he does not consider to be scientific.

[French paleontologist and philosopher] Teilhard de Chardin and his noosphere [sphere of human thought], the idea that the end of evolution is a kind of super-consciousness: not one scientific hypothesis of worth was generated from this metaphysical mayhem.

A worthwhile theory always suggests new lines of investigation, and on this criterion Darwinism has passed with flying colours. Field and laboratory studies helping us to understanding how evolution works are beyond counting. The behaviour of Darwin's finches on the Galapagos Islands has been studied for decades. A million generations of fruit flies have given up their lives to unravel the mysteries of the expression of genes. In the process many debates have opened up—like the relative importance of sex or geography in generating new species. This does not mean that Darwin is in trouble. It just means that the science is still vigorous, that understanding is honed progressively.

So that is why biologists get so mad at the propagation of ID. It wastes time. It suppresses research rather than encouraging it. It's not really a theory, it's a story. It deflects the young from asking the important questions. It serves to kill curiosity rather than encourage it. Sometimes it is right to get angry in the face of unreason. Darwinists are readily labelled. There should be an equivalent term for the proponents of Intelligent Design. May I suggest IDiots?

EVALUATING THE AUTHOR'S ARGUMENTS:

In this viewpoint, Richard Fortey argued that the theory of intelligent design cannot be tested scientifically. If this is so, do you think that the theory should be discussed in a science class? Why or why not?

Chapter 3

Should Public Schools Allow School Prayer?

Logan Thore (center) leads a student prayer group next to the flagpole at his Asheboro, North Carolina, high school on September 27, 2006. They're participating in the national "See You at the Pole" event that encourages Christians to gather outside their schools and pray.

Prayer Should Be Allowed in Schools

AllAboutGod.com

"School prayer would instill moral values."

In the following viewpoint, AllAboutGod. com explains many of the arguments in favor of allowing school prayer. They argue that school prayer supports freedom of religion, acknowledges religious heritage, and offers many benefits for society. AllAboutGod. com is the Web site of a collection of people that consider themselves followers of Jesus, rather than simply "Christians."

AS YOU READ, CONSIDER THE FOLLOWING QUESTIONS:
1. In the author's opinion, how did the U.S. Supreme Court misinterpret "freedom of religion?"
2. What does AllAboutGod.com cite as evidence that the U.S. educational system has a rich spiritual heritage?
3. What are the benefits of school prayer, according to the authors?

There are many arguments supporting the view of citizens who favor the return of prayer to public schools.

Prayer in school is constitutional and supports the principle of freedom of religion on which the U.S. was founded:

- In banning school prayer, the U.S. Supreme Court has misinterpreted the Establishment Clause of the Constitution. A simple and voluntary school prayer does not amount to the government establishing a religion, any more than do other practices common in the U.S. such as the employment of Congressional chaplains, government recognition of holidays with religious significance such as Christmas or the proclamation of National Days of Prayer.
- In banning school prayer the U.S. Supreme Court has mistaken the principle of "freedom of religion," guaranteed by the U.S. Constitution, for freedom *from* religion and any observance of it.

Illinois state representative Jonathan Wright smiles on April 1, 2002. He sponsored a bill that clarified that students in Illinois are allowed to engage in prayer in their schools at any time, and it has just passed the state House unanimously.

- School prayer would allow religious students the freedom to observe their religious beliefs during the school day. The U.S. Supreme Court has urged school cooperation with religious authorities for "it then respects the religious nature of our people and accommodates the public service to their spiritual needs."

Prayer in school acknowledges our religious heritage

- Our country was founded by people who believed in freedom to practice one's religion openly and who used their religious beliefs to create the backbone of this nation. Our children should be able to participate openly in this great heritage, seeking help, strength, and endurance from God as did their forefathers.
- Our system of education also has a rich spiritual heritage. Of the first 108 universities founded in America, 106 were distinctly Christian, including the first, Harvard University, chartered in 1636. In the original Harvard Student Handbook, rule number 1 was that students seeking entrance must know Latin and Greek so that they could study the Scriptures: "Let every student be plainly instructed and earnestly pressed to consider well, the main end of his life and studies is, to know God and Jesus Christ, which is eternal life, (John 17:3); and therefore to lay Jesus Christ as the only foundation of all sound knowledge and learning."

Prayer in school offers many societal benefits

- School prayer would instill moral values. Schools must do more than train children's minds academically. They must also nurture their souls and reinforce the values taught at home and in the community. Founding father Samuel Adams said, "Let divines and philosophers, statesmen and patriots, unite their endeavors to renovate the age by impressing the minds of men with the importance of educating their little boys and girls, inculcating in the minds of youth the fear and love of the Deity . . . and

> ### FAST FACT
>
> Sixty-nine percent of Fundamentalist Christians, 56 percent of Pentecostal Christians, and 55 percent of Evangelical Christians support opening class in public schools with a prayer.

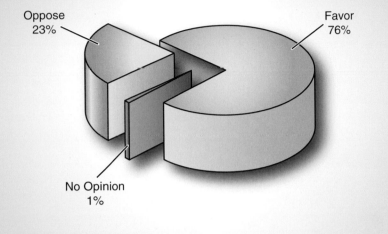

Percentage of Americans Who Favor or Oppose a Constitutional Amendment to Allow Voluntary Prayer in Public Schools

Oppose
23%

Favor
76%

No Opinion
1%

Taken from: Gallup Poll, August 8–11, 2005.

leading them in the study and practice of the exalted virtues of the Christian system."

- The public school system is tragically disintegrating as evidenced by the rise in school shootings, increasing drug use, alcoholism, teen pregnancy, and HIV transmission. School prayer can help combat these issues and is desperately needed to protect our children.

- School prayer could lead to increased tolerance and less bullying in school since it can instill a sense of right and wrong and a love for others above oneself.

- School prayer will promote good citizenship. Founding father John Adams said, "Our Constitution was made only for a moral and religious people. It is wholly inadequate to the government of any other." The founding fathers believed this should be taught in school. George Washington stated, "What students would learn in American schools above all is the religion of Jesus Christ."

- School prayer may cause students to acknowledge a power greater than themselves on which they can rely for comfort and help in times of trouble. This will lead to decreased reliance on drugs, alcohol, sex, and dangerous amusements as well as decreased suicides.

EVALUATING THE AUTHOR'S ARGUMENTS:

In this viewpoint, the author claimed that school prayer would have a number of positive societal benefits. Do you agree? Why or why not? Are there any negative consequences that would result from implementing school prayer? Explain.

Prayer Should Not Be Allowed in Schools

American Atheists

"Public schools should not be forums on behalf of religious indoctrination of any kind."

In the following viewpoint, the American Atheists argue that there should not be prayer in schools. The group claims that allowing prayer in school is likely to lead to extreme conflict among different religious and nonreligious groups about the content of the school prayer. American Atheists, a nationwide movement founded by Madalyn Murray O'Hair, which defends the civil rights of Americans who do not believe in God, works to keep church and state separate and addresses issues of First Amendment public policy.

AS YOU READ, CONSIDER THE FOLLOWING QUESTIONS:

1. What happened in Philadelphia during the "Bible Wars," according to Madalyn Murray O'Hair, as cited in the viewpoint?
2. Do religious groups today agree on school prayer, in the author's opinion?
3. What are some of the different groups that might want to have input about the content of school prayer, according to the American Atheists?

W hat happens when religions disagree? One little-known case from American history illustrates the dangers of having *any* religious exercise mandated in our public schools. . . .

Bible Wars in Philadelphia

There is a piece of American history—American religious history—which school prayer advocates do not choose to mention. This concerns the infamous "Bible wars" which erupted in Philadelphia. Madalyn Murray O'Hair discussed this obscure event in her book *Freedom Under Siege*:

> When the Roman Catholics themselves would not provide enough schools, the Catholic church turned to fight the public schools where the Catholic children were in attendance. Some people today even credit our now totally secular schools to the fact that the Roman Catholic church fought so vigorously for the removal of all the religious matter in the curriculum which might be interpreted as adverse reflection on Catholicism. Conversely, rather than have an intrusion of Roman Catholic doctrines, the Protestants agreed to secularize the schools. During the nineteenth century, then, both the Protestants and the Roman Catholics feared the influence of secular education on the faith and morals of the young people, but they each, equally, feared the theological supremacy of the other more.
>
> The road to secularization, however, was not free of difficulties or even violence. In 1844, for instance, at the urging of the local bishop, the Philadelphia school board permitted Roman Catholic children in the public schools to read from their own version of the Bible, the Douay Version. The American Protestant Association was outraged. Mass meetings were held, two Roman Catholic churches were burned, and the rioting was stopped only when the bishop ordered all his churches closed. At the church of St. Philip Neri several people were killed. The church was broken open and only the presence of the militia, the mayor and the governor prevented its being burned to the ground. . . .

Numerous other confrontations followed this incident, as competing religious sects fought over the content of school prayers or other religious instruction in public schools. In 1854, for instance, a mob attacked a Roman Catholic priest in Maine after he urged his followers to seek legal remedies against mandatory Protestant verse in the state's public schools. Fifteen years later, in 1869 there were similar confrontations in Cincinnati when Roman

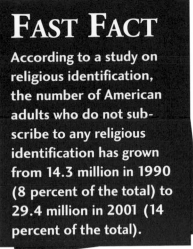

FAST FACT

According to a study on religious identification, the number of American adults who do not subscribe to any religious identification has grown from 14.3 million in 1990 (8 percent of the total) to 29.4 million in 2001 (14 percent of the total).

Catholic parents went to court in order to remove their children from religious exercises in the city's school system.

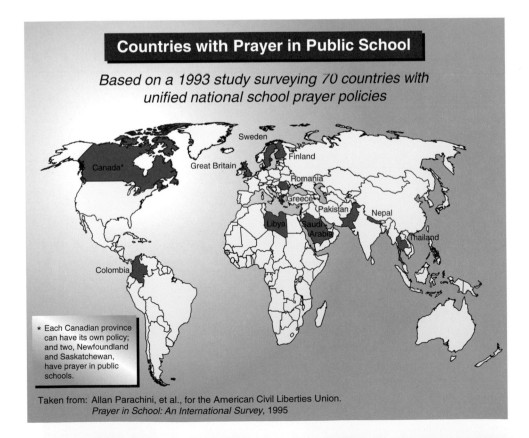

Countries with Prayer in Public School

Based on a 1993 study surveying 70 countries with unified national school prayer policies

Sweden
Finland
Canada*
Great Britain
Romania
Greece
Pakistan
Nepal
Libya
Saudi Arabia
Thailand
Colombia

* Each Canadian province can have its own policy; and two, Newfoundland and Saskatchewan, have prayer in public schools.

Taken from: Allan Parachini, et al., for the American Civil Liberties Union. *Prayer in School: An International Survey,* 1995

No Agreement on School Prayer

Especially in today's diverse culture, there seems to be little or no agreement about the exact content of the prayers which should be recited in public schools. Although fundamentalist Christians are leading the school prayer effort, many Protestant groups are skeptical, and consider the proposal a threat to religious liberty. Atheists rightly point out that any prayer violates the rights of students who have no religious beliefs.

Could we expect a repeat of the "Bible Wars"? Jews, Muslims and other religious minorities in the United State are already clamoring for "'equal access" on behalf of displays and religious events in the public square. New age cults, voodooists, satanists, spiritualists—all can insist

Lisa Herdahl (center) on her way into federal court in Oxford, Mississippi, with her son David and attorney Judith Schaefer. In 1996, Herdahl was at the center of a bitter controversy when she successfully sued to have the North Pontotoc School District end its fifty-year-old practice of school-sponsored prayer and Bible study.

on having their prayers, holy books and ceremonies incorporated into the activities of our public schools.

A modern day version of the "Bible Wars" can only divide communities and fragment parents, teachers, school boards and ultimately the students. Rather than teach values and morals, school prayer could result in confrontations over who—and what—is considered "holy". It can balkanize students into competing religious factions, and isolate the many students who have no religious beliefs whatsoever.

Religious faith—or the lack of it—should be a private affair. Public schools should not be forums on behalf of religious indoctrination of any kind. Rather than risk a twentieth century version of the "Bible Wars", communities should instead promote genuine tolerance, and ensure that schools remain educational institutions, not bully pulpits.

EVALUATING THE AUTHOR'S ARGUMENTS:

The author argued in this viewpoint that there are too many diverse viewpoints in American culture to have school prayer that would please all groups. What do you think the author would say about allowing the people to decide the issue by a vote? Explain your answer.

Schools Should Allow a Moment of Silence

Stephen L. Carter

"A moment of silence to begin the school day is an excellent compromise."

In the following viewpoint, Stephen L. Carter argues that having a moment of silence is a better option than having school prayer or nothing at all. The author claims that having a moment of silence allows religious students of all faiths to incorporate silent prayer into their school day while not forcing any students to engage in prayer. Stephen L. Carter is the William Nelson Cromwell Professor of Law at Yale Law School and writes a feature column for *Christianity Today* magazine.

AS YOU READ, CONSIDER THE FOLLOWING QUESTIONS:
1. What new Virginia statute does the author endorse?
2. What are two examples Carter cites of how states have tried to comply with the Supreme Court's decision regarding religion in school in the early 1960s?
3. Why does the author think a moment of silence is a good compromise?

Stephen L. Carter, "A Quiet Compromise: Why a Moment of Silence is Better than School Prayer," *Christianity Today,* vol. 46, February 4, 2002, p. 82. Reproduced by permission of the author.

Amid the nation's understandable preoccupation with tragedy at home and war abroad, it would have been easy to miss one of the most important stories of [2001] for the future of American schools: on October 29, the Supreme Court announced that it would not entertain a challenge to the new Virginia statute requiring a moment of silence to begin the school day.

A Moment of Silence

The law, which went into effect in the summer of 2000, was challenged as a violation of the First Amendment's prohibition on the establishment of religion. But a federal district judge dismissed the lawsuit, known as *Brown v. Gilmore*, a federal court of appeals agreed, and the Supreme Court refused to reinstate it.

Sixth grade student Leah Palmer prays at her desk during a first-period moment of silence at Northeastern Academy in Oklahoma City, Aug. 14, 2002. State law requires all schools to have a moment of silence every day.

The media gave the story very little play. If the Court is stepping out of the business of regulating moment-of-silence laws, however, that is very big news indeed.

Religious Expression Since the 1960s

Ever since the classroom prayer decisions in the early 1960s, parents who want their children to pray in school and parents who do not have been engaged in a running battle over how much religious expression to allow students, and how to avoid the appearance that the school authorities are championing religion.

The rush to avoid endorsement has led to some uncommonly silly results, like the school in New Jersey that did not allow a Christian student to read his favorite story to the class because it came from the Bible. The courts agreed with this strange decision, suggesting that the command of the First Amendment is that the government should discriminate against religious speech.

There have also been some very good compromises, like the federal statute that requires public schools to grant religious clubs the same degree of access to their facilities that they give to secular clubs. (A California school district recently tried to get around this law by banning *all* student clubs; the effort crumbled under parental pressure.)

Opinion on Religious Expression Today

But the messy heart of the battle remains prayer. Surveys indicate that the school prayer decisions, 40 years after being handed down, remain highly unpopular. Yet the decisions to ban school prayer were correct, resting on an important if rarely articulated truth: the religious education of children is both the right and the responsibility of the family. This role is older than the Constitution, and the state has no power to interfere with it.

The problem with organized school prayer was that it could too easily contradict the religious teachings of the parents. (So can many other courses of study in the schools, which is why religious parents should have the right to remove their children from

FAST FACT

In 2005, Indiana changed its law to require schools to give students a daily moment of silence.

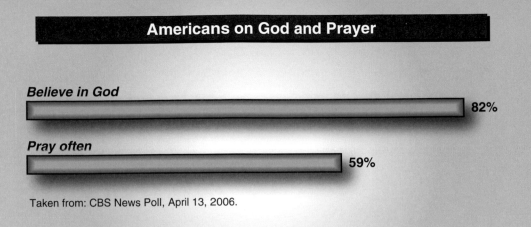

Americans on God and Prayer

Believe in God

82%

Pray often

59%

Taken from: CBS News Poll, April 13, 2006.

mandatory sex education classes, study of the theory of evolution, the ideological education that goes under the misnomer of "tolerance," and any other subject that, in parental judgment, makes it harder to raise children in the faith of the parents. . . .)

Many religious parents, however, are understandably uneasy about sending their children to schools that are aggressively secular. They want to set aside a part of the school day for their children to be fully religious, even if other children are not, without the pressure of having to sneak a moment for prayer between classes. If organized classroom prayer is not allowed, what is left to mark the work of the day as still a part of the fabric of God's creation?

A Compromise

A moment of silence to begin the school day is an excellent compromise. Although the Supreme Court in 1985 declared unconstitutional an earlier Alabama moment-of-silence statute, the grounds were flimsy: some of the legislative supporters said they hoped some students would pray, and the statute expressly authorized them to do so. (One might have thought that providing a way for students to exercise their constitutional rights was an argument *for* rather than *against* constitutionality, but evidently not.) In any case, the current law is different. The Alabama law stated that the moment of silence could be used for prayer. The Virginia law, if the distinction truly matters, does not mention the forbidden P-word.

Silence is a good thing. It gives time for prayer for those who want to pray, but it also forces everyone to take a few moments of thought, of centering, of simply slowing down in a world—especially an educational world—that moves far too fast. Beginning the school day with a respite from life's pressures is so sensible an idea that one only wishes it were more widespread.

EVALUATING THE AUTHOR'S ARGUMENTS:

The author of this viewpoint believes that his view is a good compromise. Do you think that the authors of the first and second viewpoints in this chapter would agree? Why or why not?

Restricting All School Prayer Is Unrealistic

Daniel E. Kinnaman

"For the last 35 years we've slowly, but steadily, removed references to God from our schools, and pushed prayer from the public view."

In the following viewpoint, Daniel E. Kinnaman claims that the pendulum has swung too far on the topic of school prayer. He argues that following the events of September 11, 2001, the National Day of Prayer and Remembrance was a good thing, even in public schools. Kinnaman takes the position that occasions like this show that prayer is needed at times. He claims the separation of church and state goes too far if it removes prayer completely, not allowing it on occasions such as after a national tragedy.

Daniel E. Kinnaman publishes *District Administration*, a magazine for education leaders.

AS YOU READ, CONSIDER THE FOLLOWING QUESTIONS:

1. What specific event does the author say led to prayer in public schools?
2. What examples does Kinnaman give of how the separation of church and state has gone too far?

Daniel E. Kinnaman, "God Bless America," *District Administration,* vol. 37, November 2001, p. 72. Copyright © 2001 Professional Media Group, LLC. Reproduced by permission.

3. According to the author, what position on religious expression makes America strong?

T here is a time for everything, even prayer in school.
Sometimes pendulums swing too far—at least metaphorically speaking. That's the case with prayer in public schools. The horrific terrorist attacks on our nation evoked a range of emotions, and it's hard to find anyone who would deny the value or appropriateness of a spiritual response ranking high on the list. When President [George W.] Bush proclaimed Friday, Sept. 14 [2001] a National Day of Prayer and Remembrance, no one condemned that he called on the nation to pray for the victims of the attack and to ask for God's help in seeking justice. The president didn't get cited for violating the principle of separation of church and state, but some students are wondering why it is suddenly OK to pray, even in school.

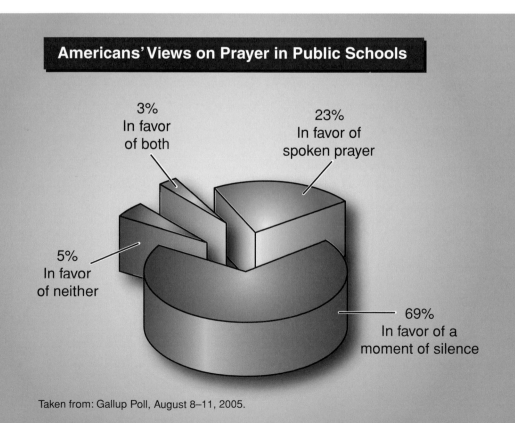

Americans' Views on Prayer in Public Schools

3%
In favor
of both

23%
In favor of
spoken prayer

5%
In favor
of neither

69%
In favor of a
moment of silence

Taken from: Gallup Poll, August 8–11, 2005.

Virtually every school in America was in session on our National Day of Prayer and Remembrance. Many let students view a broadcast of the service, and most followed the lead of Secretary of Education Rod Paige, who requested that school district leaders "consider having a moment of silence to be observed in classrooms or in a larger assembly of students."

When I asked my son what he did during his middle school's moment of silence, he told me he "just sat there." I asked him if he prayed and he said, "No, I didn't think we were allowed to pray in school." At first his response startled me, but then I realized it made perfect sense. The pendulum of prayer in school had swung too far.

For the last 35 years we've slowly, but steadily, removed references to God from our schools, and pushed prayer from the public view. In many cases this was motivated by a valid commitment to pluralism, aiming to prevent any appearance that our schools were endorsing a particular faith, or any faith at all.

Yet, for a few, the goal has been to completely eradicate religious expression from school settings. They view the separation of church and state as a license to outlaw religious expression of any kind. And over time things have gone too far.

Not enough of us questioned the sensibility of punishing students who bowed their heads at the lunch table. Somehow we bought into the idea that these alleged silent prayers were inappropriate; that somehow non-praying students would conclude that by allowing even one student to pray silently, the school was implicitly endorsing that student's religion. Out went T-shirts with scripture references and out went Christmas carols. Even jewelry with religious symbols was questioned. By the start of [the twenty-first] century, religious expression had effectively been expelled from school.

One Nation Under _____

So we shouldn't be surprised if our need and desire to express

> **FAST FACT**
>
> The Supreme Court has determined that the First Amendment requires that there be no prayer, not even nondenominational prayer, in public schools (*Engel v. Vitale,* 1962) as this would amount to unconstitutional government sponsorship of religion.

Florida secretary of state Katherin Harris offers a prayer while Governor Jeb Bush and others bow their heads, on the steps of the state capitol during the National Day of Prayer on May 3, 2001.

ourselves spiritually now confuses our students. How are they to understand the president's statement, "In time, we will find healing and recovery; and, in the face of all this evil, we remain strong and united, 'one nation under God.'" Recent valedictorians have had their speeches censored to remove such references, yet now it's a safe bet that no one will protest if God's blessing is invoked at school functions.

Despite the tragic and disastrous loss we suffered in these evil attacks, we know that good can come from it too. We've witnessed countless examples of grace and goodness. We've seen the heroism embodied in the superhuman efforts of emergency crews and rescue workers. And we've experienced unimagined compassion and generosity. Amidst all of this it's also good to see the pendulum swing back a bit toward center with regard to personal prayer and other religious expressions in school.

We now have an opportunity to teach our students the appropriate balance between the freedom of religious expression and the separation of church and state. And it's precisely this balance that makes our nation so strong. The tragedy of terrorism shows us to be a spiritual people, but we are not an indoctrinated people upon whom a fixed set of religious practices is imposed. Our enemies hate our freedom and diversity, but that is what we must celebrate and it is what we must teach to our children. They should never be afraid to say 'God bless America' and 'God bless our schools.'

EVALUATING THE AUTHOR'S ARGUMENTS:

In this viewpoint, the author claimed that prayer in school is appropriate at times. Do you agree? Why or why not? In what way might someone disagree with you?

School Prayer Disrespects the Diversity of Religious Beliefs Among Students

Thomas J. Zwemer

> *"Informed Christian citizens agree that the United States Constitution protects each one's right to pray in their own way."*

In the following viewpoint, Thomas J. Zwemer argues that bringing prescribed prayer into public schools is a mistake. Zwemer's main reason for opposing this is the diversity of religious beliefs in the United States. Zwemer points to the problem of determining what the content of the prayer would be in a nation that has members of so many faiths. He believes that better than prescribed prayer is the current constitutional protection offered to each student to have the option to pray privately in his or her own way.

Thomas J. Zwemer is vice president for Academic Affairs Emeritus, Medical College of Georgia, Augusta, Georgia.

Thomas J. Zwemer, "Teach Us to Pray," *Liberty Online,* January-February 2006. Reproduced by permission.

AS YOU READ, CONSIDER THE FOLLOWING QUESTIONS:
1. How many different religious bodies and sects are present in the United States, according to the author?
2. What is the largest single belief group, as reported by Zwemer?
3. Does the author think that no child should ever pray at school?

The increasing attempts by many "good people" to Christianize the United States by law rather than by evangelism has even reached the Supreme Court. The gospel commission given by Jesus is "Go ye therefore, and teach all nations," not "Go ye therefore, and compel all nations!" Even though we see what religion in government can do in the Middle East, many want to do the same here. The United States is one of the most devout nations in the world, and it is at the same time the most religiously diverse. The United States has more than 1,500 different religious bodies and sects—

Clergy from many different faiths gather and pray at the Cathedral of Our Lady of the Angels in Los Angeles on April 5, 2005, to mark the passing of Pope John Paul II.

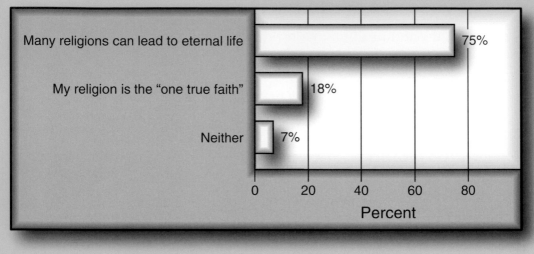

Views of Other Faiths by Religious Americans

Many religions can lead to eternal life — 75%

My religion is the "one true faith" — 18%

Neither — 7%

Percent

Taken from: Pew Forum and the Pew Research Center for the People & the Press

including 75 divisions of Baptists alone. This country has 360,000 churches, mosques, and synagogues [including independent storefront churches], all coexisting in relative harmony. There are, for example, 193 churches, synagogues, mosques, and temples listed in the Augusta, Georgia, Yellow Pages. There are five non-Christian churches listed, eleven Baptist, three Catholic, even two Presbyterian—the "right" one and the "wrong" one!

The Diversity of Prayer

More than 90 percent of Americans believe in God. More than 50 percent say they pray at least once a day, and more than 40 percent say they have attended worship services within the past week.

So it ought to be a slam dunk to bring prescribed prayer into the public schools. But here is the rub! Each believes that they alone are "right" and the prayers of other belief systems are wrong and thus ineffectual! Furthermore, each believes that support or recognition of any other "faith" is a disservice to the "truth." Thus the 10 percent who don't are the largest single group of Americans.

Just consider this: A neighbor and friend of mine is a member of the Jehovah's Witnesses and teaches public school. Colleagues of mine have wives who teach public school. Some are members of the Church of Jesus Christ of Latter-Day Saints; others are Roman Catholics, who pray to "Mary, Mother of God." Others are Unitarians, who don't believe in the Trinity or the Apostles' Creed. Still others are Muslims, Buddhists, Hindus; yet others arc agnostics. An acquaintance in Augusta who is a Christian Scientist prays to a Mother God. Which of these people would you want to compose the morning prayer for your children?

Prayer Should Be Private

Thank God and the United States Constitution, our children *can* pray in public schools. More to be praised is the fact that no one but parents or their surrogates can teach their children how to pray, or require that they listen to the prayers of others. The United States Constitution protects "captive" individuals from listening to or participating in sponsored prayer in any government-related event. Our Founders found King George's church as odious as King George's tax laws. They were of a mind that salvation is through God alone to individuals alone. Accordingly, prayer is a private conversation between the individual and God. Corporate prayer is effectual only if the group in free association is in consensus. The founders of our nation felt so strongly they fashioned the provision for the constitutional right to private prayer with equal shelter from imposed prayer.

Accusations are totally unfounded that some nefarious group moved the United States Supreme Court to deny private prayer in public places. The Court simply states that the civic right to pray and the civic right not to pray or to be part of an audience to public governmentally sponsored prayer are both protected. The Court agrees that if God does not compel, neither should the Court. Informed Christian citizens agree that the United States Constitution protects each one's right to pray in their own way.

EVALUATING THE AUTHOR'S ARGUMENTS:

In this viewpoint, Zwemer argued that the diversity of belief and nonbelief in the United States would make it impossible for any kind of mandatory school prayer. What do you think Zwemer would say to Stephen L. Carter about his suggested moment of silence? Explain your answer.

School Prayer Does Not Disrespect the Diversity of Religious Beliefs Among Students

"Jews stand to lose as much as Christians if God becomes a shameful secret."

Jennifer M. Paquette

In this viewpoint, Jennifer M. Paquette argues that school prayer is a good thing, even if the prayer is not of your own religion. The author, who is Jewish, argues against removing religion, including school prayer, from the public sphere. Jennifer M. Paquette is a Toronto-based writer.

AS YOU READ, CONSIDER THE FOLLOWING QUESTIONS:
1. Why does the author claim that it is not consistent with the Jewish faith to ban public worship?
2. Does Paquette think morality can exist without religion?
3. What is the author's answer to the worry about students of diverse faiths?

In May 2001, *Catholic Insight* (p. 23) highlighted two Jewish activists rampaging through Canadian courts, pressuring lawmakers to ban public worship. As a religious Jew, nothing could alarm me more.

The article mentioned that these secular Jews don't represent the Jewish faith; indeed, their beliefs are the furthest thing from it. Secular Jews are Jewish by culture only, but because our culture is distinct, it's too easy to abandon the faith while clinging to the externals, still claming to be "good Jews."

And they mean well. Informed by prophetic traditions, they fight injustice everywhere. But their good intentions overstep our greater goal: Judaism's task of pointing the world towards God—certainly, not away from Him.

I grew up assimilated [into the surrounding non-Jewish culture], and only began exploring Judaism as an adult in public school. I recited the Lord's Prayer, along with Catholic and Greek Orthodox classmates. At the time, I didn't realize it was Christian scripture—if I'd known, I might have remained silent. I wasn't given a choice, which is where secular Jews take issue. But, while they feel they've solved the problem, I see no cause to rejoice.

Driving Religion Out of the Public Square

Secularists claim morality can exist without religion. I believe that—like I believe a fish thrives out of water. In place of faith, schools offer bland exercises in situational morality ("Ethics and the Media"). Ontario ministry curricula claim to prepare children to "function as informed citizens . . . and . . . compete in a global economy." How low have our standards gotten, that we'll settle for *functional, competitive* children rather than *moral* and *worshipful* ones?

When my son began Grade One in a Jewish school, he complained that public school kids don't have to pray. I told him, "Even in public school, I prayed every morning." Will future

Frequency of Prayer Among Christians, Jews, and Muslims

How often do you pray?

	Christians	Jews	Muslims
More than once a day	68.1%	36.9%	91.6%
Once a day	16.1%	22.0%	3.0%
A few times a week	12.1%	27.3%	2.4%
Once a week	0.7%	4.0%	0.0%
A few times a month	1.9%	5.4%	1.8%
Once a month	0.2%	0.2%	0.0%
Every few months	0.6%	3.3%	0.6%
Not at all	0.2%	1.0%	0.6%

Taken from: Beliefnet

parents be able to say the same? Or now that daily prayer has been replaced by "meditations" from various belief systems, will they only recall fidgeting through feel-good tidbits from some teacher's self-help book of the month?

Although I shudder at having been spoon-fed Christianity, I've come to appreciate that reciting passages regularly transforms prayer into ritual, carrying us beneath familiar words towards deeper connectedness. Meditations though, render students passive—hungry bystanders at a rich banquet.

Can a moment of silence achieve the same effect? Maybe for Remembrance Day, on a regular basis, students will see it as a moment to scribble notes, fiddle with hair clips, dash off that overdue history essay; anything but reflect on their gratitude and obligation to the Source of Life.

Texas state representatives Charlie Howard (left) and Wayne Christian talk during a debate in the state House over Howard's bill to make it easier for students to voluntarily pray at school, April 30, 2007.

Addressing Diverse Faiths

Our Charter of Rights and Freedoms declares that Canada is founded upon recognition of the "the supremacy of God." But that three-letter word has become a battlefield. Are we talking about the Christian God? The Jewish *Adonay*? The Muslim *Allah*? One Hindu deity, or perhaps a multitude?

Secularists seek to eliminate this "confusion," claiming that references to God discriminate against "non-Christian and non-religious" Canadians. Jewish groups like B'nai Brith—whose name, ironically, means "Children of the Covenant"—join them, shrilly opposing "organized prayer, religious exercises, or bible classes . . . including 'moments of silence' or 'meditations' by which prayer is . . . encouraged or recommended."

Yet while B'nai Brith, and their ilk wield the mighty sword of political correctness, and school boards and governments bow down, what is the ultimate cost of their victory?

If they have their way, our children will never realize religion has a place outside of church or synagogue. Secularism robs us of the chance to proclaim our strength and uniqueness, but isn't that what diversity is supposed to be all about—not some sham "non-religion" that has become our lowest common denominator?

After [the school shootings at] Columbine, Colorado officials admitted they'd "become so fearful of affirming one religion or one value over another that [they had] banished them all." They called for a return to "faith-based morality"—not some watered-down version, but honest-to-God faith, straight up.

Our country's multiculturalism is based on a belief that we're created in God's image. How will minorities be treated here if we no longer affirm a Godly spark igniting their souls—if we're no longer permitted to even suggest they possess an eternal soul? Though secularists may hide behind Jewish banners, Jews stand to lose as much as Christians if God becomes a shameful secret. We must work together to dispel the darkness.

EVALUATING THE AUTHOR'S ARGUMENTS:

In this viewpoint the author claimed that she would rather have prayer to God in schools than no prayer, even though she is a member of a religious minority. What do you think Thomas J. Zwemer would say to Paquette? Explain your answer.

Facts About Religion in Schools

Constitutional Issues

- The "Establishment Clause" is the portion of the First Amendment that says, "Congress shall make no law respecting an establishment of religion."
- The Supreme Court has established the three requirements legislation must meet in order to be constitutional under the Establishment Clause (*Lemon v. Kurtzman*, 1971):
  1. The government's action must have a legitimate secular purpose;
  2. The government's action must not have the primary effect of either advancing or inhibiting religion;
  3. The government's action must not result in an "excessive government entanglement" with religion.

Evolution, Creationism, and Intelligent Design

- *Evolution* is a theory about the origin of life that says humans evolved from other life forms over a long period of time. Charles Darwin is the scientist credited with the theory expounded in his *On the Origin of Species*, published in 1859.
- *Creationism* is a theory about the origin of life that says humans were created by one or more supernatural beings. Various versions of creationism are found in many cultures and religions.
- *Intelligent Design* is a theory that says there is an intelligent designer behind all creation. Though the analogy had been used in earlier centuries, William Paley is one of the most renowned authors of the theory explained in his book *Natural Theology*, published in 1802.
- Evolution is not usually believed to be compatible with creationism. However, proponents of intelligent design sometimes believe in creationism and sometimes back evolution.
- The intelligent designer of intelligent-design theory does not necessarily have to be a god or any particular supernatural being (or even one), though many proponents believe the Christian god is the intelligent designer.

- A Gallup poll taken in May 2007 revealed that 43 percent of the population believe in creationism and 52 percent believe in evolution. The 52 percent of the population that believe in evolution is shared between 38 percent who believe in evolution guided by God and 14 percent who believe in evolution that involves no intelligent designer or god.

Prayer in Schools

- In the 18th, 19th, and early 20th centuries, it was customary for public schools to open with an oral prayer.
- While the Supreme Court has determined that public schools may not force students to engage in any particular prayer (*Engel v. Vitale,* 1962), the Court has never argued that students may not engage in voluntary private prayer.

Public Schools

- A form of public education was in existence in the seventeenth century in the New England colonies and was largely influenced by the religious views of the Puritans and the Congregationalists. Due to the diversity brought about by the influx of people of different religions, private schools became the norm by the middle of the eighteenth century.
- Thomas Jefferson was the first American leader to suggest the creation of a public school system, and his ideas helped to create the national system of formal education developed in the nineteenth century.
- Sentiments that were anti-Catholic and anti-Jewish in textbooks used in public schools led to the existence of separate Roman Catholic and Jewish schools in the mid-nineteenth century.
- When states finance the education of students in private schools, it is known as a school voucher program.
- Charter schools are public schools (owned publicly and publicly funded) that are run independently of the local school district.

Religion

- According to a 2001 American Religious Identification Survey performed by The Graduate Center at City University of New York, 77 percent of the U.S. population identify as Christian. Among this group, however, there are numerous different Christian religions, including (in order of popularity) Catholic, Baptist, Methodist, Lutheran, Presbyterian, Pentecostal, Episcopalian, Mormon, Church of Christ, Jehovah's Witness, Seventh-Day Adventist, and over twenty others.

- The same 2001 study found that 4 percent of the U.S. population identify with a non-Christian religion. This group includes (in order of popularity) Jewish, Muslim, Buddhist, Unitarian, Hindu, Native American, Scientologist, Baha'i, Taoist, and over ten others.
- The same 2001 study found that 14 percent of the U.S. population identify with no religion, which includes those who are atheist (believe there is no God), agnostic (have no beliefs about the existence or nonexistence of God), and others who identify with no religion.
- The same 2001 study found many differences in religious identification in states across the country:
  - While 51 percent of people in the state of Rhode Island identify as Catholic, only 6 percent of those in Tennessee do.
  - In the state of Mississippi, 55 percent of people identify as Baptist, while in Utah only 2 percent identify as Baptist.
  - In Washington state, 25 percent identify with no religion, while in North Dakota only 3 percent identify with no religion.

Organizations to Contact

American Atheists

PO Box 5733, Parsippany, NJ 07054-6733
(908) 276-7300
e-mail: info@atheists.org
Web site: www.atheists.org

American Atheists is dedicated to working for the civil rights of atheists, promoting separation of state and church, and providing information about atheism. It publishes *American Atheist* magazine and has published over 120 books, including Madalyn Murray O'Hair's *Why I Am an Atheist.*

Americans United for Separation of Church and State

518 C St. NE, Washington, DC 20002
(202) 466-3234
e-mail: americansunited@au.org
Web site: www.au.org

Americans United for Separation of Church and State is a nonsectarian and nonpartisan group whose purpose is to protect separation of church and state by working on a wide range of pressing political and social issues. It publishes the magazine *Church & State* and also produces issue-papers and reference materials.

Answers in Genesis

PO Box 510, Hebron, KY 41048
(859) 727-2222
Web site: www.answersingenesis.org

Answers in Genesis is an apologetics (i.e., Christianity-defending) ministry, dedicated to enabling Christians to defend their faith with a focus on providing answers to questions surrounding the book of Genesis. It publishes the magazine *Answers,* as well as numerous books and booklets available in print and online.

The Discovery Institute—Center for Science & Culture (CSC)
1511 Third Ave., Suite 808, Seattle, WA 98101
(206) 292-0401
e-mail: cscinfo@discovery.org
Web site: www.discovery.org/csc
The Center for Science and Culture is a Discovery Institute program that supports research by scientists and other scholars challenging various aspects of neo-Darwinian theory and developing the theory of intelligent design. The CSC also encourages schools to focus more on the weaknesses of the theory of evolution in science education. The Discovery Institute has numerous papers, policy positions, and videos available, including *Teaching About Evolution in the Public Schools: A Short Summary of the Law.*

First Amendment Center
1207 Eighteenth Ave. South, Nashville, TN 37212
(615) 727-1600
e-mail: info@fac.org
Web site: www.fac.org
The First Amendment Center works to preserve and protect First Amendment freedoms through information and education. The center serves as a forum for the study and exploration of free-expression issues, including freedom of speech, of the press, and of religion as well as the rights to assemble and to petition the government. It publishes a number of pamphlets, including *Teaching About Religion in Public Schools: Where Do We Go from Here?* and *Religious Liberty, Public Education, and the Future of American Democracy: A Statement of Principles.*

Freedom from Religion Foundation
PO Box 750, Madison, WI 53701
(608) 256-8900
e-mail: info@ffrf.org
Web site: www.ffrf.org
The Freedom from Religion Foundation is an educational group working for the separation of state and church. Its purposes are to promote the constitutional principle of separation of state and church, and to educate the public on matters relating to nontheism. It publishes the

newspaper *Freethought Today*, as well as several books and brochures such as *The Case Against School Prayer.*

Institute for Creation Research
10946 Woodside Ave. North, Santee, CA 92071
(619) 448-0900
e-mail: info@icr.org
Web site: www.icr.org
The Institute for Creation Research works to equip believers with evidence of the Bible's accuracy and authority through scientific research, educational programs, and media presentations, all conducted within a biblical framework. It publishes *Acts & Facts*, a monthly news booklet dealing with creation, evolution, and related topics.

Intelligent Design and Evolution Awareness (IDEA) Center
PO Box 1742, San Diego, California 92177-7424
(858) 337-3529
e-mail: info@ideacenter.org
Web site: www.ideacenter.org
The IDEA Center is a nonprofit organization dedicated to promoting intelligent design theory and fostering good-spirited discussion and a better understanding about intelligent design theory and the creation/evolution issue among students, educators, churches, and anyone else interested. The center publishes many articles on its Web site, including *The Science Behind Intelligent Design Theory.*

National Center for Science Education (NCSE)
20 Fortieth St., Suite 2, Oakland, CA 94609-2509
(510) 601-7203
e-mail: ncseoffice@ncseweb.org
Web site: www.ncseweb.org
The National Center for Science Education defends the teaching of evolution in public schools and gives advice to keep evolution in the science classroom and creationism out. The NCSE publishes *Reports of the National Center for Science Education*, or *RNCSE*, which gives wide coverage of all aspects of creation/evolution issues.

National Council on Bible Curriculum in Public Schools (NCBCPS)
PO Box 9743, Greensboro, NC 27429
(877) 662-4253
Web site: www.bibleinschools.net
NCBCPS aims to bring a state-certified elective Bible course into the public high schools nationwide. It publishes a newsletter and has published a book, *The Bible in History and Literature.*

For Further Reading

Books

Bruce J. Dierenfield, *The Battle over School Prayer: How* Engel v. Vitale *Changed America*. Lawrence: University Press of Kansas, 2007. A guide to the first court case that addressed the constitutionality of prayer in public schools.

Joan DelFattore, *The Fourth R: Conflicts over Religion in America's Public Schools*. New Haven, CT: Yale University Press, 2004. Traces the evolution of school-prayer battles from the early 1800s, when children were beaten or expelled for refusing to read the King James Bible, to current disputes over prayer at public-school football games.

William Dembski and Michael Ruse, eds., *Debating Design: From Darwin to DNA*. Cambridge: Cambridge University Press, 2004. Provides a comprehensive balanced overview of the debate concerning biological origins covering four positions: Darwinism, self-organization, theistic evolution, and intelligent design.

Norman Geisler, *Creation and the Courts: Eighty Years of Conflict in the Classroom and the Courtroom*. Wheaton, IL: Crossway, 2007. Offers a behind-the-scenes look at the testimonies and arguments of the prosecution and defense of the major creation versus evolution court battles.

Kent Greenawalt, *Does God Belong in Public Schools?* Princeton, NJ: Princeton University Press, 2004. Asks what role religion ought to play in public schools. The author explores many of the most divisive issues in educational debate, including teaching about the origins of life, sex education, and when—or whether—students can opt out of school activities for religious reasons.

Frank S. Ravitch, *School Prayer and Discrimination: The Civil Rights of Religious Minorities and Dissenters*. Boston: Northeastern University Press, 2001. Asserts that current legal discourse over prayer in the public schools, which centers the issue around First Amendment rights, underestimates the ways in which school prayer fosters discrimination against religious minorities and dissenters.

Raymond R. Roberts, *Whose Kids Are They Anyway? Religion and Morality in America's Public Schools*. Cleveland: Pilgrim, 2002. Shows how proposals for moral education in public schools are shaped by definitions of religion and argues that public education's critics overstate the failures of public education.

Gordy Slack, *The Battle over the Meaning of Everything: Evolution, Intelligent Design, and a School Board in Dover, PA*. Hoboken, NJ: Jossey-Bass, 2007. In this eyewitness account of the twenty-first-century courtroom drama in Dover, Pennsylvania, that put evolution on trial, the author offers a firsthand account that details six weeks of some of the testimony—a battle between hard science and religious conservatives wishing to promote a new version of creationism in schools.

Stephen D. Solomon, *Ellery's Protest: How One Young Man Defied Tradition and Sparked the Battle over School Prayer*. Ann Arbor: University of Michigan Press, 2007. The story of how one student's objection to mandatory school prayer and Bible reading led to one of the most controversial court cases of the twentieth century, *Abington School District v. Schempp*, a decision that still reverberates in the battle over the role of religion in public life.

R. Murray Thomas, *God in the Classroom: Religion and America's Public Schools*. Westport, CT: Praeger, 2007. Explores conflicts over the teaching of evolution, inserting the word *God* in the Pledge of Allegiance, conducting school holiday celebrations, posting the biblical Ten Commandments in schools, and praying at school functions by looking at their historical and cultural contexts.

Periodicals

Jerry Adler et al., "Doubting Darwin: How Did Life, Its Infinite Complexity, Come to Be? A Controversial New Theory Called 'Intelligent Design' Asserts a Supernatural Agent Was at Work," *Newsweek*, February 7, 2005.

Jonathan Alter, "Monkey See, Monkey Do: Offering ID as an Alternative to Evolution Is a Cruel Joke. It Walks and Talks Like Science but in the Lab Performs Worse than Medieval Alchemy," *Newsweek*, August 15, 2005.

America, "Religious Worship in Public Schools," July 21, 2003.

Americans United for Separation of Church and State, "Prayers Dropped from S.C. High School Graduation," *Church & State*, July 1, 2003.

Kurt Andersen, "Backward, Christian Soldiers! Why Must Intelligent Design be Stopped? Because This—God Forbid—Could Be the Moment When the Theocratization of America Makes a Real Advance," *New York*, October 17, 2005.

Neela Banerjee, "Divided over Evolution: Darwin's Theories Are Nearly 150 Years Old, but the Debate over How Schools Should Teach the Origins of Life Continues," *New York Times Upfront*, March 28, 2005.

Rob Boston, "Devious Design," *Church and State*, November 2003.

David Brooks, "One Nation, Enriched by Biblical Wisdom," *New York Times*, March 23, 2004.

Sarah Childress, "See You in Bible Class: Georgia Plans to Teach the Good Book in Schools," *Newsweek*, May 1, 2006.

Christianity Today, "Uncle Sam's Prayer Stick: Educators Can No Longer Afford to Ignore Federal Guidelines on Religion in Schools," April 2003.

Current Events, "Reading, Writing, and Religion? A Debate of Biblical Proportions," March 4, 2005.

Kenneth C. Davis, "Jefferson, Madison, Newdow?" *New York Times*, March 26, 2004.

Melissa Deckman, "Holy ABCs! The Impact of Religion on Attitudes about Education Policies," *Social Science Quarterly*, June 2002.

Lorna Dueck, "Schools and Religion Do Mix," *Globe & Mail* (Toronto), April 5, 2006.

Christian de Duve, "From the Big Bang to the Origins of Life," *Nation*, October 23, 2006.

Economist, "The Origin of Life: How Life Got Going. Maybe," February 18, 2006.

Shaunti Feldhahn, "Schools OK with Season, Not Reason,"November 17, 2004.

Richard T. Foltin, "Religion in Education: Consensus and Conflict," *Human Rights*, Summer 2006.

Jeremy Harding, "What to Wear to School," *London Review of Books*, February 19, 2004.

Dan Hardy, "Jesus Costume Banned by School Gains Some Support in Abington," *Philadelphia Inquirer*, February 25, 2007.

Charles C. Haynes, "From Battleground to Common Ground: Religion in the Public Schools Doesn't Need to Be a Flash Point for Controversy If Your District Has Crafted Policies and Exercises Them," *School Administrator*, October 2006.

Todd Huffman, "Intelligent Design Not Testable: It Can't Be a Scientific Theory, *Eugene (OR) Register-Guard*, July 9, 2006.

Nick Jackson, "Against the Grain: 'There Are Strong Indications of Intelligent Design,'" *Independent* (London), February 8, 2007.

Robert W. Lee, "Essay on Religious Freedom," *New American*, May 5, 2003.

Gilbert S. Omenn and Alan I. Leshner, "No Conflict Between Science and Religion," *Witchita (KS) Eagle*, July 30, 2006.

H. Allen Orr, "Devolution," *New Yorker*, May 30, 2005.

Eyal Press, "Darwin on Trial," *Nation*, November 28, 2005.

Debra Rosenberg, "A Family and a Flag: Behind the Pledge Case Lies a House Divided," *Newsweek*, March 29, 2004.

Charles J. Russo, "Of Baby Jesus and the Easter Bunny: Does Christianity Still Have a Place in the Educational Marketplace of Ideas in the United States?" *Education & Law Journal*, July 2006.

Teen People, "Pledge of Allegiance: For Decades Students Have Saluted the American Flag at School with the Words "One Nation under God." Does the Country's Commitment to the Separation of Church and State Require That the Religious Reference Be Dropped?" May 1, 2005.

Terrence Tilly and John Rowe, "Evolution Fight Not About Origins of Life: Science Cannot Address Some Issues," *Dayton (OH) Daily News*, September 19, 2005.

Claudia Wallis, "The Evolution Wars: When Bush Joined the Fray Last Week, the Question Grew Hotter: Is "Intelligent Design" a Real Science? And Should It Be Taught in Schools?" *Time*, August 15, 2005.

Eugene G. White, "The Absence of Daily Prayer," *School Administrator*, October 1, 2006.

Robert Winder, "God, Allah or the Flying Spaghetti Monster: With

Right Wing Christians on the March, Robert Winder Asks If There's Any Place for Creationism in the Classroom," *Chemistry and Industry*, January 2, 2006.

Web Sites

Objectivity, Accuracy, and Balance in Teaching About Religion (www .teachingaboutreligion.org). This Web site is designed to assist teachers of middle and high school history and social science classes in their handling of religion—including nonreligion—as curricular subject matter.

Ontario Consultants on Religious Tolerance (www.religioustolerance .org). This Web site contains many articles on different religions of the world, as well as comparative essays and opinion essays. The site also contains links to other sites involving religion.

Pew Forum on Religion and Public Life (pewforum.org). The Pew Forum on Religion & Public Life, launched in 2001, seeks to promote a deeper understanding of issues at the intersection of religion and public affairs. The Web site has numerous polls and reports about these issues.

Index

United States. *See* America, American

University of North Carolina, 10

Utah, 102

Vaccines, 65

Violence, 28, 76

Virginia, 37, 80, 83

Voodooists, 78

Washington, D.C., 19

Washington, George, 73

Washington (state), 60, 102

Western civilization, 37

White supremacy, 11

"Why Evolution Is Stupid", 53, 55

Why I Am an Atheist (O'Hair), 103

Worship, 19, 96

Yale University, 80

Picture Credits

Cover: Reproduced by permission of photos.com
All photos © AP Images